Corporate Communication and Integrated Marketing Communication

INTEGRATED MARKETING COMMUNICATION

Series Editor: Jeanne M. Persuit, University of North Carolina Wilmington

Integrated marketing communication (IMC) is a holistic approach to the areas of advertising, public relations, branding, promotions, event and experiential marketing, and related fields of strategic communication. This series seeks to ground IMC with communication ethics in order to take the theory and practice of IMC beyond a critical and deconstructive understanding and into new areas of productive inquiry. We seek to advance the scholarship of IMC in a manner that influences and informs future practice. Submissions may rely on varied methodologies and relate to the study and practice of communication and its theoretical diversity, including but not limited to the areas of rhetoric, visual communication, media ecology, philosophy of communication, mass communication, intercultural communication, and instructional communication. We welcome submissions addressing all facets of IMC and its relationship with communication ethics. While edited volumes will be considered, we encourage the submission of scholarly monographs that explore, in depth, issues in IMC as related to communication ethics.

Titles in the Series

Corporate Communication and Integrated Marketing Communication: Audience beyond Stakeholders in a Technological Age by Christina L. McDowell Marinchak and Sarah M. Deluliis

Integrated Marketing Communications in Risk and Crisis Contexts: A Culture-Centered Approach by Robert S. Littlefield, Deanna D. Sellnow, and Timothy L. Sellnow

Integrated Marketing Communication: Celebrity and the American Political Process by Jennifer Brubaker

Sport Teams, Fans, and Twitter: The Influence of Social Media on Relationships and Branding by Brandi Watkins

Integrated Marketing Communication: Creating Spaces for Engagement edited by Jeanne M. Persuit and Christina L. McDowell Marinchak

Corporate Communication and Integrated Marketing Communication

Audience beyond Stakeholders in a Technological Age

Christina L. McDowell Marinchak
Sarah M. DeIuliis

LEXINGTON BOOKS
Lanham • Boulder • New York • London

Published by Lexington Books
An imprint of The Rowman & Littlefield Publishing Group, Inc.
4501 Forbes Boulevard, Suite 200, Lanham, Maryland 20706
www.rowman.com

86-90 Paul Street, London EC2A 4NE, United Kingdom

British Library Cataloguing in Publication Information Available

Library of Congress Cataloging-in-Publication Data

Names: McDowell Marinchak, Christina L., author. | DeIuliis, Sarah M., author.
Title: Corporate communication and integrated marketing communication : audience
    beyond stakeholders in a technological age / Christina L. McDowell Marinchak, Sarah
    M. DeIuliis.
Description: Lanham : Lexington Books, [2023] | Series: Integrated marketing
    communication | Includes bibliographical references and index. | Summary: "In
    this book, the authors trace corporate communication and integrated marketing
    communication (IMC) historically and situate industry practices today to draw
    attention to the need for companies to reach audiences beyond traditional
    stakeholders"— Provided by publisher.
Identifiers: LCCN 2023014498 (print) | LCCN 2023014499 (ebook) | ISBN
    9781498566827 (cloth) | ISBN 9781498566834 (epub)
Subjects: LCSH: Business communication. | Communication in marketing. | Customer
    relations.
Classification: LCC HF5718 .M4314 2023 (print) | LCC HF5718 (ebook) | DDC
    658.45 $2 23/eng/20230418—dcundefined
LC record available at https://lccn.loc.gov/2023014498
LC ebook record available at https://lccn.loc.gov/2023014499

To our families . . .

Contents

Acknowledgments

We offer many thanks and gratitude to *all* those who helped us throughout the writing of this book.

First, we thank our editor, Jessie Tepper, and former editor, Nicolette Amstutz from Lexington Books/Rowman & Littlefield. Your patience and assistance through this process were most appreciated.

Second, we offer thanks and appreciation to graduate student, Michaela Christensen, who provided her reference support for this project.

We thank the Integrated Marketing Communication series editor, Jeanne M. Pursuit, for supporting this project.

Christina offers her thanks and appreciation to her co-author, Sarah, for her inspiration, encouragement, support, and most of all the blessing of her friendship. Sarah also offers her thanks and appreciation to Christina for her many years of friendship, leadership, support, and grace.

With endless gratitude, we offer our thanks and appreciation to our families, who offer continual support and wisdom. Christina dedicates this book to her husband, Marc, and her son, Noah. Sarah dedicates this book to her husband David, her son, Dominic, and her daughter, Gianna. We dedicate this book to them because they are what matter the most.

Introduction

Uniting Corporate Communication and Integrated Marketing Communication: An Introduction to Understanding Audiences beyond Stakeholders in a Technological Age

In today's historical moment, understood in the context of a technological environment that arguably defines, redefines, and shapes communication practices both publicly and privately, uniting the practices of corporate communication and integrated marketing communication (IMC) is of the utmost importance to begin to engage with the audiences that are impacted by messaging in the marketplace. In an era defined by branding, two-way communication, and immediate gratification, many popular culture and industry examples illustrate the necessity of understanding audiences beyond stakeholders in a technological age. As recently as November 2022, the need for brands, companies, and organizations to engage with audiences beyond traditional stakeholders continues to be an area of attention and concern.

In November 2022, Ticketmaster, a website for public sale of event tickets, took to Twitter to announce to the public: "Due to extraordinarily high demands on ticketing systems and insufficient remaining ticket inventory to meet that demand, public on-sale for Taylor Swift | The Eras Tour has been cancelled" (Ticketmaster). The chaos over the cancelled ticket sales not only left "Swifties" red with bad blood, but forced the U.S. government to enter the conversation. Public outcry and conversation included a Senate subcommittee, which "[held] a hearing on the lack of competition in the ticketing industry," requests for the Federal Trade Commission (FTC) to enforce laws designed to fight the use of "bots" online ("bot attacks"), and fans to sue

Ticketmaster over the cancelled sale (Kelly 2022). The Taylor Swift concert ticket sales is just one of many examples of the integration of stakeholders (i.e., fans), audiences (i.e., music consumers), and publics (i.e., social media users) in corporate, organizational, and brand messaging, and opens a path to discussing uniting corporate communication and IMC in a technological age.

We contend that the integration of corporate communication and IMC practices is of the utmost importance and necessary to meet the demands of all audiences who impact organizational life. We refer to key terms throughout this book to guide our discussion of corporate communication and IMC unification, including "stakeholder," "audience," and "publics." We refer to Freeman (2010) for the definition of a traditional *stakeholder* as "any group or individual who can affect, or is affected by, the achievement of the corporation's purpose" (vi). Stakeholders include employees, managers, and other internal groups responsible for shaping the brand. A stakeholder is also different from a shareholder underscored by Friedman (1962) recognizing "the corporation is an instrument of the stockholders who own it" (135). For the purposes of this book, we borrow the definition of audience from IMC literature, as this is a place that IMC informs corporate communication practices. We define *audience* as any person who is the intended reader and hearer and/ or has the potential to interact with a message (Shirky 2008). Audience is also discussed in industry via a number of terms (i.e., public relations [publics], advertising [audience], marketing [target markets]). Finally, we turn to Grunig (1997) for our definition of *public(s),* specifically a "public latent,"— a group that is "in many distant social issues but actively concerned about those issues that affect it directly" (16). The terms "stakeholder," "audience," and "public(s)" provide an interpretive opening to discussing the uniting of corporate communication and IMC in a technological age.

In adopting these key terms, this book specifically considers the current and relevant communication strategies adopted by companies and brands alike that specifically assist organizations in navigating a complex environment comprised of a multitude of channels to guide messaging toward audiences. Dominating that environment today are the technology (e.g., social media) platforms and sites that contain within them a plethora of professional, personal, public, and private forms of communication coming from a vast array of peoples, industries, and circumstances. Kamal (2022) notes that "fast-moving consumer trends are urging marketers to be bolder in their approach, sparking more data-led campaigns and more audience-centric storytelling. On top of that, brands now have a host of channels at their fingertips, from social media to email marketing, from brand awareness campaigns to Google ads" (Kamal 2022). Adopting a "bold" communication strategy while simultaneously acknowledging the variety of channels through which influence and impact can occur illustrates the power of corporate communication and IMC in today's historical moment.

More importantly, however, through these various media, the *number* of people with potential to be influenced and impacted has increased significantly and transcended the traditional stakeholder model so often adopted in corporate communication and in IMC practices. Kamal (2022) offers strong branding examples that respond specifically to this new turn in a complex communication environment. One of those examples is Duolingo, a language-learning technology company headquartered in Pittsburgh, Pennsylvania, that has gained interest and notoriety for its strong branding practices over the social media platform TikTok. Duolingo routinely posts content through their channel where their mascot, Duo the owl, participates in TikTok trends and comments on pop culture current events. Kamal asks, "If you're wondering how this relates to people learning a new language, the answer is it doesn't really. But that's kind of the point. At its core, successful content marketing doesn't explicitly promote products, but it stimulates an *interest* in a product, service, or brand" (Kamal 2022). Importantly, Kamal notes that this communication strategy has been *so* successful that the content has inspired "user-generated content" that has framed this "online community" as a powerful lesson (Kamal 2022). In this historical moment, learning how to speak to audiences beyond traditional stakeholders creates an opportunity for even stronger brand positioning.

Understanding brand identity and reputation finds foundation in corporate communication practices. The standard way of thinking about a company's corporate communication strategy involves *planning* communication with stakeholders (e.g., employees, customers, investors). According to Argenti (2006), "within companies, the term *corporate communication* is used to describe four distinct aspects of communication," including a "function," "channel of communication," "communication process," or "an attitude or set of beliefs" (358). Argenti suggests that many different elements of corporate communication, as it relates to aspects of communication, have impact for audiences beyond stakeholders. First he says, "a company's corporate communication function is responsible for communication with both internal and external stakeholders" and a number of subfunctions, including "media relations, investor relations, internal or employee communications, government relations or public affairs, community relations, corporate philanthropy, corporate reputation, and marketing communication" that will be touched on throughout the book (358). Second, Argenti (2006) makes the point that corporate communication channels include both information in print and online, noting that the communication process consists of the "style of communication, including tone and timing" that aligns with organizational culture (e.g., informal or formal) and, furthermore, the beliefs and attitudes inherent in the communication process itself (358). Corporate communication from an IMC perspective includes these aspects of communication, however, and moves beyond traditional stakeholders by considering a multiplicity of audiences.

Today we live in an age of increasing technological connection influencing how companies communicate with audiences. The change in the technology environment is accelerating the need for companies and brands to decide when, how much, and with whom information is shared. When it comes to the topic of corporate communication and IMC, most scholars and industry professionals will readily agree that technology has changed practices. However, in acknowledging this changing landscape, one might ask why moving to audiences beyond stakeholders yields positive impact for companies and brands today. Our aim is to suggest ways for understanding audiences beyond stakeholders with the hope of uniting corporate communication and IMC. This book attempts to bring together corporate communication and IMC through a human communication connection within an organizational context—specifically, how companies and brands can be effective in reaching internal and external audiences in their communication in a technological age. Human communication relies on historicity, or the understanding that a historical moment answers questions of communicative patterns. Arnett and Arneson (1999) note that "communication is a process guided by persons, text, and the historical moment . . . because communication is an ever-changing process, we cannot divorce our communicative understanding from the historical moment of interpretation" (31). For Arnett and Arneson (1999), human interpretation is tied to the moment that the communication emerges from. More specifically, within society, human beings are constantly changing. Without addressing the constraints of the moment, one cannot understand the communicative demands that moment also puts forth.

Thomas Kuhn (1996), in *The Structure of the Scientific Revolution*, points to the importance of historicity, which acknowledges that progress and progression toward a goal does not happen with flat, linear events but with deeper understanding of historical implications. Within the field of communication, understanding the importance of a historical moment in regards to the questions that face humanity and society is exceptionally important to appreciating and understanding how individuals respond to those questions. Kuhn (1996) suggests that paradigms tell us things about culture and society positioned within a particular time frame. Paradigms, then, show human beings where they have gone and can offer coordinates for the future.

Arguably, corporate spaces can create, reconstruct, or reify paradigmatic shifts. One specific area this communication takes place is with consumptive practices adopted by the marketplace. Today, it is commonplace to understand the symbiotic communicative relationship between consumption and identity. According to Mary Douglas and Baron Isherwood (1996), in their text *The*

World of Goods: Towards an Anthropology of Consumption, goods provide a means to "make and maintain social relationships" (39). The authors continue, "Goods, then, are the visible part of the culture. They are arranged in vistas and hierarchies that can give play to the full range of discrimination of which the human mind is capable. The vistas are not fixed; nor are they randomly arranged in a kaleidoscope. Ultimately, their structures are anchored to human social purposes" (44). Therefore, through the act of consumption, identities are created, sustained, and communicated (McDowell Marinchak and Burk 2016).

For example, bleisure travelers were named a top-ten trend shaping the hospitality industry in 2022 (Weisskopf and Massett n.d.). Bleisure traveling refers to a current shift in the public sphere where remote employees have started to travel throughout the year *while* still working full-time. This means that the hospitality industry sees a boost in tourism but, and simultaneously, must begin to provide spaces for work environments. As Weisskopf and Massett (n.d.) note, "this is a great opportunity for hotels and F&B venues to capitalize on the trend and adapt their offering to meet the needs and wants of this emerging segment." Essentially, the identity of the remote employee allows for a new market to emerge where companies in the hospitality industry have the opportunity to provide new messaging to respond to audience needs and wishes. This could not be done, however, without acknowledgment of corporate values, audience communication, and marketing strategies. Furthermore, acknowledging this new market identifies a new communication need to speak to audiences beyond traditional stakeholders so as to offer new opportunities to never-before identified audiences.

In this work, we take up the call to uniting corporate communication and IMC by beginning with one basic assumption. Today's communication environment demands the acknowledgment that those audiences who receive and are influenced by messages from companies transcend traditional stakeholders. In a moment where the connection between consumption and identity is further compounded by communication technologies and social media platforms, corporate communication and IMC practices, when united, offer an ethical and pragmatic way of reaching audiences. Branding efforts communicate corporate values and identify and reflect that in both corporate communication and IMC practices.

We offer a constructive hermeneutic approach to building an argument for consolidating corporate communication and IMC in an effort to better understand audiences. This work proceeds through five chapters that frame a new perspective on audiences in light of a complex communication environment. Postmodernity is a historical moment marked by narrative and virtue contention and opens up the opportunity to learn from difference (Arnett, Fritz, and

Bell 2009). According to Ronald C. Arnett (2005), "postmodernity assumes that pragmatic necessity of encountering clashing rhetorics that represent differing narrative traditions with dialectic giving insight into alterity and dialogue permitting the meeting of difference" (2). A postmodern perspective allows for the multiplicity of perspectives provided within the work.

In chapter 1, we offer a brief summary of the historical development of both corporate communication and IMC. Our analysis situates both communicative practices, but simultaneously proposes important coordinates for uniting the practices in decision-making by companies. Chapter 2 considers the important relationship between rhetorically engaging audiences within an understanding of communication ethics. Because companies reach audiences that transcend traditional stakeholders at a mass scale, the relationship between persuasion ethics is an essential factor in developing a perspective sensitive to the unification of corporate communication and IMC. In chapter 3, we offer an overview of the relationship between organizational culture and the implementation of corporate communication and IMC practices. Organizational culture, furthermore, must fully support the connection between corporate communication and IMC to attend to audiences beyond stakeholders. Chapter 4 suggests that this work is impacted most directly by the complex communication environment that has been shaped by communication technologies. We consider a brief perspective on media ecology that, furthermore, shapes a textured response to corporate communication and IMC in a technological age. In chapter 5, we apply the theoretical foundation provided in this text to a current case study in the social media strategies practiced by Duolingo. As noted by Kamal (2022), Duolingo serves as a noteworthy example of the unification of corporate communication and IMC in a technological age.

Through this framework, we consider the importance of strategic communication that is sensitive to the human person who exerts brand loyalty and influence in the public sphere. As Barnett Pearce (2007) in *Making Social Worlds: A Communicative Perspective* suggests, "all of us create worlds that are 'complete' or 'whole' within their own horizons and that are structured by a geometry of 'oughtness' that tells us what things mean and what we should, could, must, or must not do about or because of them" (49). He expresses, a person's social worlds are where "speech acts, episodes, and forms of communication, same and forms of consciousness, and relationships and minds are made"; this is the place where we coordinate actions and management/ make meaning (101). Human beings are all connected by similar things like genes, language, opinions, desires, family structures, and so on, but people are only in relationships that they name for themselves (2007). With this, people "do not organize their lives around things; rather they use things to communicate order and organization in their lives" (Groom 2008, 15). While it is true people engage in social circles in which consumption patterns are relatively similar, they also have a greater reach in the public sphere today that permits greater influence on companies and brands (beyond those in which they have a stake).

Companies and brands *must* communicate frequently and engage audiences while simultaneously being prepared to embrace technological changes. In doing so, companies and brands communicate a willingness to not only provide information on platforms used by stakeholders but meet them there and audiences beyond. This book hopes to offer a way to unite corporate communication and IMC, reaching audiences beyond stakeholders, by better understanding the human communication relationships people have with companies and brands in a technological age. To begin, we start with the historical developments of corporate communication and IMC to move towards making the necessary shift to communicating with audiences beyond traditional stakeholders.

Chapter 1

A Historical Perspective of Corporate Communication and Integrated Marketing Communication

This work begins with a historical overview and analysis of corporate communication and integrated marketing communication (IMC), approached through a humanities and interpretative perspective. By reviewing the history and practices of corporate communication and IMC through this lens, this work examines the theoretical and applied management of communication in for-profit and not-for-profit corporate settings critical for organizational success at all levels. Importantly, this historical overview and analysis also provides contextual and narratival background for understanding the necessary shift that has been made and that continues to *need* to be made to communicating with audiences beyond traditional stakeholders. The historical evaluation of corporate communication and IMC demonstrates the importance of attending to the changing communicative landscape particularly as the public sphere shifts and changes based upon consumer expectations and demands. Importantly, we do not claim a comprehensive historical overview of both disciplines, as the development of each area is complex and situated across many decades. However, the historical dynamics and themes of this evolution situate this project's focus on audience in this historical moment.

Today, corporate communication and IMC, though centered upon communication by and about a company, focus on various aspects of a public communicative structure. Corporate communication is driven by the company within (decisions are made internally) and communicated to stakeholders. IMC emphasizes changing behavior in consumers, not just attitudes and expectations. The changing communicative landscape of the corporate environment necessitates response, which can be achieved through uniting both corporate communication and IMC. Being responsive to this changing

1

environment creates opportunity to engage in and with particularly valuable communicative strategies for reaching audiences beyond traditional
stakeholders. Throughout this chapter, we will address the expectations and
attitudes of consumers. However, those expectations and attitudes translate
to behaviors and communicative patterns engaged by consumers that impact
companies and brands alike.

This chapter argues that corporate communication and IMC exist in the
current scholarship as (often) bifurcated areas of inquiry and practice. More
specifically and traditionally, scholars address corporate communication and
IMC as separate areas, and industry professionals take on the role of tech-
nicians, or specialists in their respective areas (e.g., public relations). The
intent is to find a common ground for corporate communication and IMC
scholarship in which to address the previously mentioned bifurcated position,
proposing an alternative constructive approach to IMC. To begin to answer
how companies can coordinate communication through integrated efforts, we
begin with a historical analysis of both corporate communication and IMC
to provide a clear view of the bifurcated state of the two areas. Moreover,
it provides the structural rise of internal and external communication in the
marketplace with clear coordinates and markers for corporate communication
and IMC in a technological age.

This chapter proceeds with a historical overview and analysis of corporate
communication; a historical overview and analysis of IMC; and a discussion on the current bifurcated state of corporate communication and IMC
with attention directed toward implications for today's marketplace. More
specifically, offering a history of corporate communication and IMC presents
a ground from which to understand the current communicative environment
and landscape that necessitates a responsiveness to audiences beyond traditional stakeholders. The rise of communication technologies, increasing communication between consumer and company, and changing behaviors from
consumers impact the constraints and structure of organizational communication. No longer top-down communicative patterns, companies and brands
must adhere to such an environment. Looking at its historical development
provides a textured response to current demands.

HISTORICAL OVERVIEW AND ANALYSIS
OF CORPORATE COMMUNICATION

We begin with corporate communication to contextualize the development of
internal communications as well as identity and mission, both of which are
intricately connected to branding practices in IMC. According to the *Oxford
English Dictionary*, the word "corporate" derives from the Latin *corpus,*

meaning "body" ("Corporation"). Corporate communication is the total communication of a company and the messages disseminated (Christensen, Torp, and Firat 2005). For many communication scholars, particularly in corporate communication, the focus is that "all forms of communication must be orchestrated into a coherent whole," which, furthermore, means that any "success criteria" must be "developed" with an eye toward understanding the measurable outcomes of the impacts of "organization's communication on its reputation and value" (Van Reil and Fombrun 2007, 36). Accordingly, "all corporate communication begins with notions of communication strategy" (Argenti 1996, 88; Munter 1992). Strategic corporate communication highlights a need to understand the entirety of the function of organizational communication as it impacts a company's public (and often private) reputation.

As Argenti (1996) points out, the interpretative standpoint that corporate communication manifests with strategy can be traced back to Aristotle's three-part system that Aristotle defined in *Art of Rhetoric* in terms of speech which includes "a discussion of 'the speaker, the subject of which he treats, and the person to who is addressed'" (88). Argenti reviews scholars throughout his work in considering corporate communication, and in particular, Mary Munter (1992). Munter (1992), in *A Guide to Managerial Communication*, discusses a similar theoretical ground for corporate communication, tying it back to communication strategy. Though her work is in relation to management communication, Munter posits that strategic communication relies upon "variables" that include "(1) communicator strategy . . . (2) audience strategy . . . (3) message strategy . . . (4) channel choice strategy, including when to write and when to speak; and (5) culture strategy, including how cultural variations affect your strategy" (Argenti 1996, 88; Munter 1992, viii). Through Munter's work, Argenti (1996) contends this theory of management communication can be (and should be) applied to corporate communication (88). Corporate communication, as a strategy, blends together sender, receiver, message, media, and culture to effectively represent organizational values and mission.

Holistically, corporate communication emphasizes the set of activities in a company that focuses on the managing of communication to internal and external audiences beyond the traditional stakeholder. Van Riel and Fombrun (2007) consider corporate communication, as a theoretical construct, to be the key communicative framework that draws together corporate and organizational entities with their audiences (and, more particularly, stakeholders) (14). Extending beyond that initial linkage from company to traditional stakeholders, corporate communication makes up marketing communications, organizational communications, and management communications (22). The integrative nature of corporate communication provides a foundation for companies to streamline communication internally, but to also move out of the organizational network and extend messaging to audiences that transcend traditional stakeholders, consumers, and audiences.

The field of corporate communication has developed throughout the twentieth century in companies (Argenti 1996). Argenti (1996) notes, "Although corporations had no specific strategy for dealing with communications as a functional area earlier this century, they often had to respond to external and internal constituencies whether they wanted to or not" (75). From Argenti's (1996) perspective, with changing social, political (e.g., laws), and economic climates as well as advances in technology, companies have no choice but to lend attention and carefully attend to public communication with audiences, particularly in light of what the historical moment calls for and invoking the notion of "historicity" articulated in the introduction of this text (see Arnett and Arneson 1999). For example, the 1970s marked a shift in corporate communication practices that were accompanied by societal changes and new perspectives, ultimately leading companies to develop specific functional areas (i.e., a corporate communication department) in its business practices (75).

Argenti (1996) comments that, in its earlier stages, corporate communication was practiced as a tactical function used by companies to respond to the social shifts and was labeled as public relations (PR) or public affairs (75). These tactics were preventive measures to keep problems from coming in or going outside of the company and used to specifically protect company leaders, an approach known as the "flak era of public relations" due to the shielding tactics industry professionals used to prevent companies (e.g., top management) from eternal attacks on the place and its people (76). As demand for more internal and external communication with a variety of audiences increased, the role of public relations expanded beyond building and maintaining a public image for a company. Particular practices, like speech writing and company newsletters, propelled corporate communication into an area of study in schools of communication and journalism before moving into the business and management communication areas (76). This shift into the "flak era of public relations," coupled with study in schools, focused corporate communication into a needed area of business strategy requiring "real expertise" (76). It was because of this development that the role of the communication professional becomes a more standardized and publicly needed addition to corporate life.

As companies began to recognize the importance of addressing more complex communication situations, and sought the advice of communication professionals, an opportunity emerged for the opening of public relations firms (e.g., external consulting). Public relations "operated as outsourced communications departments for many organizations who could not afford their own or who needed extra help for special situations, such as crisis or promotional activities" (Argenti 1996, 76–77). Furthermore, an increasingly changing communication environment prompted the increase in external issues, necessitating organizational response and solidifying an organizational need to develop and maintain internal PR industry professionals (77). A public sphere characterized by an increasing demand for organizational responsiveness created the need for more business-oriented specialists who could navigate both a media-saturated environment and the human communication extending beyond it (77).

The expansion of corporate communication as a practice led to the development of subfunctions beyond media relations. As Argenti (1996) notes, the areas of modern corporate communications functions include image and identity, corporate advertising, media relationship, financial communications, employee relations, community relations and corporate philanthropy, government relations, and crisis communication (77). Cornelissen (2017), an expert in the area of corporate communication, emphasizes the four most important "specialist areas" emergent in companies: "media relations, employee communication, issues management and crisis management" (155). To summarize, media relations involve working with and "managing communication with the media—all writers, editors, and producers who contribute to and control what appears in print, broadcast and online news media" (155); employee relations traditionally were defined as "communication with employees internal to the organization." However, in today's technological age, "messages to employees do not always remain inside the company" and "blurred the boundaries between 'internal' and 'external' communication" (175); issue management is a proactive approach by companies and "involves scanning and monitoring the environment and detecting potential and actual issues" (209); and crisis communication is the communication response companies put in place "to effectively respond to crisis scenarios when they emerge" (213). While this is not an exhaustive list, the aforementioned practices represent the major corporate communication functions/specialist areas of a large company.

As the 1970s and 1980s gave way to the 1990s and beyond, corporate communication continued to gain traction in internal communication departments *and* serve an external branding function for audiences and stakeholders alike. Moving into our current historical moment, Van Riel and Fombrun (2007) outline the responsibilities of corporate communication:

- to flesh out the profile of the "company behind the brand" (corporate branding);
- to develop initiatives that minimize discrepancies between the company's desired identity and brand features;
- to indicate who should perform which tasks in the field of communication;

- to formulate and execute effective procedures in order to facilitate decision-making about matters concerning communication;
- to mobilize internal and external support behind corporate objectives. (23)

Through these strategic responsibilities, corporate communication offers clear parameters for internal communicative opportunities and challenges, while simultaneously framing and structuring the guidelines for potential external communication, an essential factor in discussing the bifurcated state of corporate communication and IMC. Van Riel and Fombrun (2007) note that corporate communication, as a practice, adopts a comprehensive perspective that permits the practices to be "meaningfully positioned within the interdisciplinary research and educational field of management" (23). The opportunities offered in the overlap of communication across all areas of an organization are significant.

The historical development of corporate communication, particularly within the last century, offers significant coordinates for understanding the current marketplace and the communication expectations coming from audiences across the public sphere. Without doubt, whether internal or external, structuring messages that are effective and appropriate is key to corporate communication strategy. Messages developed externally are specifically influenced and guided by the internal communication practices of any given brand or organization. In order to fully understand the holistic view of organizational communication today, this work turns now to IMC to further understand the development of strategic communication for organization and brands today.

HISTORICAL OVERVIEW AND ANALYSIS OF IMC

Current trends in IMC practices emphasize responding to changing *behavior* in consumers, and not just responsiveness to the changing of attitudes. Therefore, in thinking about business practices from an IMC perspective, companies must identify audiences beyond stakeholders as both behaviors and attitudes are influenced extensively beyond the immediate messages coming from organizations. Organizational decision-making, furthermore, should consider the communicative implications of their general decisions insofar as audiences beyond traditional stakeholders are empowered and have access to information unlike ever before. As a whole, IMC integrates the areas of advertising, public relations, promotions, marketing communication, direct marketing, event and experiential marketing, and online marketing. Because of the extensiveness of an IMC practitioner's purview, very little option remains; IMC necessitates the call to engage audiences beyond the stakeholder. Such reframing initiates a dialogic approach within the communication that provides an alternative for understanding the importance of integrating all areas within a company.

The practice of IMC emerged out of the decades of the 1980s and the 1990s as a particular approach to communication and dialogue between brand and consumer. In the late 1980s, new and rapid technological changes, especially across digital platforms, a new focus on branding and brands, and increased globalization opened up a discussion around IMC as an important theoretical idea (Schultz and Schultz 2004, 9). Rehman, Gulzar, and Aslam (2022) note that IMC was practiced as early as 1991 (5). Schultz, Tannenbaum, and Lauterborn (1993) marked a turning point in marketing communication, and their work quickly became a hallmark for both academic studies of IMC as well as the practice and implementation of IMC as a whole. At the time of the work's appearance, advertising was the major form of top-down interaction *from* brand *to* consumer, where branding practices were not nearly emphasized as much as a focus upon product or service (Schultz and Schultz 2004). However, with the rise of communication technologies—particularly at the onset of the 1990s—this concept quickly changed, as companies could no longer function without an integrated approach to generating brand recognition and brand loyalty.

IMC pioneers Schultz and Schultz understand IMC as a "strategic business process used to plan, develop, execute, and evaluate coordinated, measurable, persuasive brand communication programs over time with consumers, customers, prospects, and other targeted, relevant external and internal audiences" (Schultz and Schultz 2004, 20–21). IMC is a holistic approach to understanding how a company communicates with its audiences (McDowell Marinchak and Burk 2016). The movement from a traditional marketing product focus to a contemporary marketing consumer focus allows for greater integration across marketing platforms and greater understanding of the communication interactions that take place on the customer journey from initial interaction with a brand, to purchasing from a brand, to (hopefully) long-term brand loyalty.

IMC places particular emphasis on communicative messages, making possible the integration of marketing communication efforts that emphasize the necessity of one voice, one message, and one sound in all messages being sent to an intended audience (Schultz and Schultz 2004, 23). The one voice and one message mantra of IMC manifests as finding voice and generating consistent messaging across a multitude of channels that meet various audiences in the public sphere. IMC practitioners, attempting to advance awareness of products, services, and brands, find audiences not just in the traditional models of top-down information, but through IMC's commitment to two-way communication between brand and audience. This necessitates attending to consumer attitudes, behavior, and psychology (which will be detailed later in this work).

Seeing humans as complex, decision-making creatures problematizes the one-way, top-down communication approach from organization to consumer and elevates the unique communicative capacity held by human beings (McDowell Marinchak and Burk 2016). IMC understands the dialogical nature and ongoing message exchange between brand and customer, uniquely grounding IMC in the communication discipline (McDowell Marinchak and Burk 2016). Furthermore, understanding communication theory as IMC's theoretical ground allows for a more ethical and effective business practice (Persuit 2013, 43). IMC's theoretical development has permitted current practices to be grounded in practical consideration for the IMC efforts of organizations, particularly as they connect to culture.

Kerr et al. (2008) point to the 1989 definition from the American Association of Advertising Agencies (AAAA). The AAAA defines IMC as "a concept of marketing communications planning that recognizes the added value in a programme that integrates a variety of strategic disciplines—e.g., general advertising, direct response, sales promotion and public relations—and combines these disciplines to provide clarity, consistency, and maximum communication impact" (qtd. in Kerr et al. 2008, 515). Kerr et al. (2008) add strategic emphasis on the move from customers to a variety of stakeholders and, in addition, focus on long-term brand loyalty as a strategic communicative goal in IMC practices for all brands, with particular emphasis on the expansion of messaging to include all interaction points between an audience member and that given company or organization (516). Kerr et al. (2008) provide a comprehensive literature review to emphasize that IMC is not a new concept, including important scholarship from Duncan (2002) and Hartley and Pickton (1999); however, what is new in the IMC process is the addition of communication technologies that have further complicated the process of maintaining stakeholder relationships, making explicit integration of mission and values (corporate communication) with identity and external reputation (IMC) necessary.

Other scholars articulate that the rise of the popularity of IMC, particularly in this historical moment, can be attributed to its "inclusiveness—bridging the study of practitioners and organisations, bridging perception and behaviors" (Ots and Nyilasy 2017, 492). More specifically, Ots and Nyilasy (2017) note that IMC is a *practice theory*, meaning that it is exists through the literal practices of industry professionals, implicitly emphasizing the human element of IMC as a field (493). The authors explore the development of IMC academically, and articulate several key elements that are accepted by practitioners, namely holistic integration of key messages that rely upon comprehensive communication strategies and professionals (495). This turn also invokes the connection between marketing practices and corporate communication programs.

Duncan (2004) posits that IMC focuses on a *"one voice, one look"* mindset that is responsive to a set of required practices that respond to the consumer mentality in each given moment. Some of those include, but are not limited to:

> All customer touch points impact the brand and brand equity, not just advertising and promotional messages;
>
> Interactive, two-way communication is just as important as one-way mass media messages;
>
> Transactions are "relationship" building blocks—each transaction strengthens or weakens a customer-brand relationship . . .
>
> Retaining and growing customers is just as important, if not more so, than acquiring customers. (5)

For Duncan, the emphasis on two-way communication and relationship building demonstrates a particularly important IMC factor that is manifesting now more than ever in today's marketplace. With respect to consumer behavior, this emphasis directly impacts consumer decision-making, often outside of the direct control of organizational messaging.

Bartholomew (2017) laments a new push for modern marketing that obscures the presence of advertising messages. Because of communication technologies, Bartholomew notes that organizations are developing practices that allows companies to push into spaces where traditional advertising has historically not been seen. He suggests that these spaces allow for companies to "develop rich and portable records of consumer preference, deliver advertising customized for the idiosyncratic thought processes of individual commercial targets, and obscure their own role by mobilizing others to convey their advertising messages for them" (2). Because of the influx of advertising and marketing messages, coupled with an increase in access to the personal and private behaviors of consumers (thanks to channels such as social media data), companies must develop unique practices to meet the expectations of consumers. Bartholomew critiques these methods, noting that advertisers in particular must increasingly depend upon spaces that were often left untouched by the industry, which he notes is a direct result of the communication technologies that continue to influence the public sphere (27–28). Because of this, IMC has become almost inescapable, and furthermore consumers are turning further and further away from traditional efforts. This influx of messaging, as described by Bartholomew, illustrates the impacts these forms of communication have upon audiences beyond traditional and immediate stakeholders.

Given this, albeit short, historical overview of the practices and theoretical development of IMC, several key components emerge that will direct and structure the rest of this work. First, a changing technological landscape provides the same opportunities for a company's message to reach and impact a multitude of audiences regardless of whether or not they belong to a traditional stakeholder group. Second, because messaging impacts so many varied audiences, companies and brands experience both a new responsibility and a new call to consider *all* communication in terms of its impact on those same audiences. Maintaining ignorance of impact on audiences beyond stakeholders is not an acceptable pattern of communication and messaging. Thirdly, just as consumers now became active shapers of the messages that they receive *because* of communication technologies, companies also have greater access to information about the demographics and psychographics that influence consumer behavior. Therefore, this work examines ethics as foundational to this move to audiences beyond traditional stakeholders. Finally, given IMC's focus on relationship building, companies are called to a new responsibility to attend to the maintenance of those relationships, including cultivating and protecting brand loyalty through attentiveness to all stakeholders and audiences alike.

THE BIFURCATED STATE OF CORPORATE COMMUNICATION AND IMC

This work begins with these historical discussions of corporate communication and IMC to draw attention to the need to turn to audiences outside of the traditional parameters of stakeholders. Because this turn is necessitated by consumer behavior, this work also directly addresses the bifurcated state of corporate communication and IMC, and considers the importance of both areas in connection to one another. In drawing upon the historical overview of both practices, what remains clear is that there is a clear linkage between corporate mission and values to brand identity. While the practices of corporate communication and IMC have been historically divided into separate areas of organizational communication life, their implications heavily impact one another.

Authors Alwi et al. (2022) provide an extensive literature review on the connections between IMC (which they refer to as marketing communication, or MC) and corporate communication (referred to as CC). The authors note that both areas speak, by and large, for *all* communication efforts coming from organizations to their various constituents. In reviewing the current scholarship, Alwi et al. suggest that "rather than communicating IMC or CC separately, an organization needs to consider a more holistic approach to brands when communicating to all of its stakeholders, as these concepts are inseparable because an organization's brand messages derive from both managerial and organizational core values" (408). They call this approach "total communication," and note that, though corporate communication and IMC tend to focus on separate elements of an organization, they are necessarily connected, bridging IMC's focus on advertising and marketing with corporate communication's focus on the need to reach a variety of stakeholders over both internal and external issues (408). Via this perspective, true integration of messaging is possible, keeping the notion of identity at the center of communication and business practices.

Other voices offer caution to this conversation. Belasen and Belasen (2019) push for a theory of an *integrated* corporate communication approach while simultaneously recognizing the concern from others about singularity of voice (i.e., Christensen, Morsing, and Cheney 2008; Johansen and Andersen 2012) (368). The polyphony of scholarship moves Belasen and Belasen to suggest that integration should consist of unification of messaging with a singular identity, perhaps comprised of a multitude of values or voices (369). This perspective, strategically, allows for an "audience-driven business process of strategically managing stakeholders, content, channels, and results of brand communication programs," which include those programs found in IMC and corporate communication practices (369). Moreover, in their work, Belasen and Belasen recognize that corporate communication is "no longer the exclusive domain of PR or marketing departments, which traditionally focus on" IMC efforts—those departments have expanded to include a wide variety of departments with vested interests in both internal and external practices (369). In their analysis, and through the various threads of scholarship that they weave together, these authors *also* paint a united picture of corporate communication and IMC as different yet necessarily overlapping.

Thus, in recent years, a bifurcated state between corporate communication and IMC is collapsing. Moreover, given the historical overview of both areas, a humanities perspective suggests that *human* communication and interpretation on branding, brand values, and corporate identity are driving consumer behaviors and practices. This work will take up this collapse and offer unique touchpoints to understand this move. The next chapter, which highlights audience and the role of communication ethics in understanding audience, offers an understanding of the notion of audience *beyond* traditional stakeholder definitions in light of the historical overview provided in this chapter. Understanding the background of the development of these fields offers an entrance into the reconceptualization of audience that adequately and accurately meets current consumer behaviors in the public sphere today.

Chapter 2

Audience and Communication Ethics

March 2020 is often colloquially referred to as the unofficial start of the Covid-19 pandemic. Importantly, during this time frame, stay-at-home orders were issued and in-person interaction became increasingly rare. Both publicly and privately, human communication shifted to *only* virtual as communication technologies became the singular option to remain connected with one another. Significantly for corporate communication and IMC practices, the globe transitioned into virtual working environments that continue as hybrid working environments as of the writing of this book. Virtual spaces became essential for the marketplace to continue to operate. Yet, as the globe remained under orders to stay at home, brands became conduits through which community might still possibly be made and, significantly, adopted messaging as part of their communication strategies that acknowledged the uncertainty that the entire world faced.

In this moment, companies and brands had a significant challenge in maintaining the bottom line but also a unique opportunity to engage in communication toward and with audiences beyond immediate stakeholders. IKEA, for example, rose to that opportunity. Its campaign, #StayHome, launched in Spain and focused on actively pushing the global message to not leave the home during the initial outbreak of the Covid-19 pandemic. Arenci (2020) noted that the campaign "avoids a direct sales message" and yet had been seen by over 1 million people on Twitter at the time of his article. Like other companies at the time (e.g., McDonald's, Nike, Heinz, Dove), IKEA promoted a call for accepted safety measures that aligned with its core business practices, launching an "e-catalogue" with family games and interesting articles called "Family Boredom Solutions" (IKEA). In that moment, IKEA did not communicate *just* to its immediate stakeholders. Rather, the company delivered a campaign that transcended the bottom line. By doing so, it strengthened its brand position in ways that speak to the overall goal of corporate communication and IMC.

The IKEA example demonstrates both a responsiveness to the communication environment but also illustrates a moment in which a company responded to an audience need both rhetorically and ethically, once again reflecting the notion of historicity (Arnett and Arneson 1999). Christopher Tindale (2013), while writing about the importance of audience in argumentation, notes that "we are always 'in audience,'" that we, as a public sphere, are routinely shaped by culture and society (509). This includes in both face-to-face as well as virtual environments. If we are always in an audience, a company's and brand's communication practices *must* understand that audience no longer simply refers to a target public. Furthermore, culture and society impact audience behavior and attitude, two factors that companies and brands must consider in messaging practices.

This chapter focuses on audience in corporate communication and IMC practices by overviewing the term "audience" from a rhetorical perspective and communication ethics lens; analyzing the impact of the rhetorical and ethical audience in corporate communication; addressing the expansion of audience in IMC practices; and offering implications for communication strategies in a marketplace characterized by communication technologies. As we consider the importance of audience beyond traditional stakeholders, we also recognize the important factors of culture and technology that influence this shift. However, prior to articulating the roles that culture and technology play on communication practices, we first seek to understand the communication ethics implications of audiences adapting to our current historical moment. This framing of audience, while responsive to the description discussed in the "introduction" of this work, expands this definition to provide a rhetorical and ethical lens that situates the need to attend to traditional audiences beyond stakeholders.

THE AUDIENCE: UNDERSTANDING PUBLICS RHETORICALLY AND ETHICALLY

While understanding audience in the current historical marketplace is essential, audience adaptation is an ancient practice that traces its roots with the rise of rhetoric. This section specifically draws attention to important themes in the rhetorical scholarship in antiquity that continue to resonate with corporate communication and IMC practices today. This overview is certainly not exhaustive. Rather, we seek to situate an understanding of audience rhetorically to begin to understand the interplay of this coordinate with communication ethics and the influence of both on corporate communication and IMC.

Aristotle (*antiquity*) understood rhetoric to mean "an ability, in each [particular] case, to see the available means of persuasion" (37). As this section will demonstrate, audience adaptation was a key factor in the ancient development of the practice and study of rhetoric, and rhetorically engaging audiences is an essential factor in all corporate communication and IMC practices today.

The study of rhetoric can be traced to antiquity, when scholars were concerned about participation in the public sphere and in culture, seeking to develop strong citizenry. At that time, the concern over the rhetorical emergence of oral and literary communication (i.e., Havelock 1963) introduced an element of audience adaptation with significant implications for corporate communication and IMC practices. Havelock (1963), whose primary scholarly focus centers upon this interplay of orality and literacy, considers Plato's arguments on rhetoric through Plato's rejection of poetry. Havelock (1963) contended that Plato's critique of poetry centered upon the problems of opinion, which directly linked to his concern of sophistry being based in manipulation, rather than truth and knowledge. For Havelock (1963), Plato emphasized a need to truthfully persuade an audience, or to help an audience to find truth and knowledge, by both effective means *and* by considering the audience itself (their needs, interests, etc.). A person who merely memorizes the opinions of others loses the ability to discern and to attend to tradition, an audience, and truth. This is further complicated in our historical moment in which knowledge is sought through a multitude of media.

Aristotle (*antiquity*) takes up the study of rhetoric, paying particular attention to its practical application and requiring adaptation to the needs of the audience in order to persuade. In his *Rhetoric* (350 BCE), Aristotle notes that a rhetor should consider audience in terms of cultural norms, emotions, age, and social class. Furthermore, Aristotle notes three persuasive appeals that adapt to the audience—logos (appealing to reason), pathos (appealing to emotion), and ethos (appealing to character/credibility). Aristotle was specific in that all three appeals are directed toward *an audience* (*antiquity*). Rhetorically, then, acts of persuasion depend upon human communication and an audience in order to effectively achieve their purpose.

Rhetorical engagement of audiences becomes even more important in a technological age, in which a multitude of audiences beyond traditional stakeholders raise their perspectives in the public sphere. For example, in late 2021, Starbucks workers at a New York store voted to unionize, making it the first time for the company. Since then, Starbucks has been "fighting back against the union push" and is focusing on repairing its employee relations (raises, trainings, benefits, etc.; Lucas 2022). At the center of this communication, however, is the conversation around unfair labor practices on the internet and social media. The unfair labor practices conversations demonstrate the significant impact orality and literacy in a technological age can have on a company's decisions and audiences in its corporate communication and IMC practices.

Though Plato and Aristotle are two scholars in a centuries-long development of the nature of rhetoric, these voices begin the ancient practice of attending to audiences when attempting to persuade, to communicate, and to engage with others. Since Plato and Aristotle's contributions, the idea of rhetoric has been applied to a multitude of contexts and with a number of different voices. While this chapter considers this important implication for corporate communication and IMC as we expand what it means to be an audience of a company or a brand, we also take seriously Plato's concerns about rhetoric as manipulation. Taking Plato and Aristotle as our starting point, we turn to a discussion of communication ethics to continue to provide a place to unite corporate communication and IMC in an attempt to respond to audiences beyond traditional stakeholders.

Understanding audiences rhetorically calls forth a need to learn from communication ethics to further engage audiences beyond traditional stakeholders. Scholars interested in communication ethics focus on holding human beings responsible and accountable for their communicative behaviors and actions. This is the starting point for ethical engagement of each other. Working with people from different perspectives from one's own, a person gains an understanding of the importance of enacting virtues in life to experience the fullness of an enriched life. The goal in discerning the correct action or choice is that virtuous actions are engaged, invoking both a virtuous responsiveness *and* engaging of concern for others. Engaging in such actions, and attempting to make the correct choices under this framework, often leads to enacting what is best for people, and can thereby be a means to reaching excellence.

Scholars and theorists have postured communication ethics as a grounding framework for which ethical judgment and principles are constructed for a given audience (e.g., Aristotle *antiquity*, MacIntyre 2007, Schrag 1986). These ethical structures constitute standards for which to improve not only upon a person but upon society as a whole. This gives attention to the need for a communication ethic that would propel society *forward*—to improve upon society in multiple ways, including a common ground of acknowledging what is "protected and promoted" by society that would provide a framework for perpetual movement (Arnett, Fritz, and Bell 2009, 4).

A common ground as an approach to beginning to bridge differences/perspectives can be constructed, defined, and refined through a process of behaviors, ideas, and attitudes that are attributable to the collective thought of an audience. Human meeting has great power. When contact is made with particular people, this can have a tremendous impact on others and reshape us; our life can be changed as a result of unplanned events. With the development of these ideas as well as the moments in which conceptualizations of what is protected and promoted, the moral and the ethical emerges, and a communication ethic is developed that is particularly attentive to recognizing and engaging *difference*, relying heavily on the communicative ideal of finding common ground.

Today's postmodern society is characterized by competing narrative structures as well as extreme and varied differences that permeate boundaries and cultures (Taylor 1989). This makes common ground difficult to achieve. A communication ethic provides a solution for finding enough commonality to move beyond difference in today's society. A human being is called to recognize and engage difference, announcing respect for the narratives that shape and inform any human being's worldview. Traditional audiences, understood within corporate communication and IMC frameworks, are also called to participate in this action by choosing to support (or not to support) a company or brand. In this way, a communication ethic also calls for an audience member to "bracket" the actions of a company or brand in particular moments (Arnett and Arneson 1999, 39). For example, in November of 2022, Balenciaga, a luxury brand conglomerate, revealed two ad campaigns that sparked allegations that the brand "condoned child exploitation" (Paton, Friedman, and Testa 2022). The one campaign "featured photos of children clutching handbags that look like teddy bears in bondage gear. Another campaign featured photos that included paperwork about child pornography laws" (Paton, Friedman, and Testa 2022). Balenciaga made a public statement and deleted all campaign ads; however, as a result, if consumers want to continue to purchase the goods and services from brands owned by Balenciaga, they will need to bracket Balenciaga's choices, thus pointing to an ethic for moral judgment and decision-making. Adopting a communication ethic approach in the public sphere also calls a company and brand to recognize and engage difference as part of the shared identity in which audiences (e.g., consumers) participate. A common ground that allows various and diverse perspectives to meet in communication offers an opportunity to respectfully encounter other people.

Finding common ground through difference embraces a communication ethic committed to the building of a community of practice. Such commitment is a promise to a narrative, which is particularly important for companies and brands when navigating the communicative landscape that impacts relationships with audiences today. Focusing on building consumer relations is vital in order to fulfill the parameters of corporate communication and IMC when approached through the lens of communication ethics. A company should strive to move away from prioritizing itself over its audience in order to remain attentive to communication ethics. For example, in September and

October of 2022, the Try Guys, a group of four men who began their career together on YouTube, were forced to make significant business decisions in the wake of scandal. One of the founding members, Ned Fulmer, was caught in a cheating scandal with an employee after having branded himself for years as a family-oriented man. Significantly, the remaining three members of Try Guys made the decision to remove Ned from the group, including all branding and communication efforts. They also issued an apology on behalf of Try Guys, the brand (Press-Reynolds 2022). Recognizing common ground amongst audiences and companies also places demands upon a company and brand to uphold the given ethical judgments deemed appropriate by its audiences and *not* the company.

In *Professional Civility: Communicative Virtue at Work* (2013), Janie M. Harden Fritz frames *telos*, or an end of activity, as part of human flourishing being connected back to the workplace. Fritz grounds her claim in the work of Alasdair MacIntyre (2007), who engages virtue ethics as a communicative path toward upholding a "professional ideal" that finds roots in both professional "history and tradition" (2013, 30). Our communicative actions set up guideposts (or rules to live by) that shape the narrative coming from people or institutions (e.g., company codes of ethics). Specifically, *telos* for human beings, as an end, calls forth a virtue ethics approach that allows for human qualities to guide communicative action. Fritz's project centers upon professional civility, which she calls a "communicative virtue" that understands *telos* to support particular goods of the professions, which include productivity, place, and persons (8). In promoting social responsibility, what is relevant becomes real, and the workmanship of a company becomes vital to its people and to its surroundings. Lessening the focus on the company and building consumer relations, then, helps establish real connections between a person and others in communicative encounters.

In keeping with Fritz's work that unites communication ethics, virtue, and professional life, Tanni Haas (2001) discusses the question of management through a lens attentive to communication ethics. Haas considers the interplay of organizational communication with the varied audiences that may or may not transcend traditional stakeholders. For Haas, organizational decision-making must account for a number of different values, interests, and stakes, including those of audience members; unfortunately, those same "interest claims" can be "based on different, and potentially mutually conflicting, underlying values" (423). Haas brings forth an understanding of what it means for a company/person to treat all audiences in an ethical way. Haas turns to scholars such as Jürgen Habermas, who addresses similar issues in the public spheres. Scholars like Haas have looked to Habermas's discourse ethics, and his ideal speech situation, for ideas for solving these kinds of ethical issues that begin to point to the need to attend to audiences transcending traditional stakeholders.

Habermas's discourse ethics on a conception of self-other relations that requires, as Haas suggests, the company (the self) to work together with its audiences/publics (the others) by abstracting their interests from the values in which they rest (2001). In Haas's (2001) estimation, the company and audiences *must* take their interests down to a subtle stage in which both parties' views are considered valuable. Returning to Plato and Aristotle, speaking to audiences requires a rhetorical skill set that cannot act without ethical considerations. To move rhetoric beyond manipulative persuasion requires a sensitivity to human *telos*, decision-making, interests, and values that, while not united in total agreement, must be attended to in a marketplace driven by communication, dialogue, and the merging of competing interests, especially in a technological age.

In *Here Comes Everybody: The Power of Organizing without Organizations* (2008), Clay Shirky explores how technology, specifically through social interaction, changes the way people form and exist in groups. Shirky's work provides the basis for our definition of audience—any person who is the intended reader and hearer and/or has the potential to interact with a message. In today's technological society, audiences have both power and size (106). Shirky posits:

> Every new user is a potential creator and consumer, and an audience whose members can cooperate directly with one another, many to many, is a former audience. Even if what the audience creates is nothing more than a few text messages or e-mails, those messages can be addressed not just to individuals but to groups, and they can be copied and forwarded endlessly. (106)

Technology affords industry professionals the opportunity to reach audiences beyond traditional stakeholders. As Shirky writes, "All businesses rely on the managing of information for two audiences—employees and the world" (107). With the internet and other social outlets, reaching both internal and external audiences has become relatively simple, but managing disseminated information is no easy task. The constant changes in the technological landscape make it increasingly challenging for companies and brands to stay ahead of both internal and external audiences in its messaging. This section's attention to a rhetorical audience viewed through a communication ethics lens pushes the need to unite corporate communication and IMC practices even further to strengthen relationships with audiences beyond traditional stakeholders. This chapter now turns to corporate communication and IMC to draw out implications for companies reaching audiences in a technological age.

CORPORATE COMMUNICATION:
ENHANCING INTERNAL AUDIENCES

In the practices of corporate communication and IMC, understanding audience is arguably be one of the most essential components of strong and sound integration of corporate communication and IMC as corporate philosophies. More specifically, and as will be discussed in subsequent chapters, the influx of communication technologies has *forced* industry professionals to consider audiences beyond traditional stakeholders. Communication technologies have, in essence, expanded the very definition of audience. Literature reviews of corporate communication (e.g., Cornelissen 2017) and IMC (e.g., Laurie and Mortimer 2019) provide a succinct review of the definitions, yet each definition offered acknowledges an audience-focused component to successful implementation of these practices.

Tindale (2013) suggests that we respond to both the moment and the environment in a way that is shaped by our worldview, and we recognize that messaging requires our receptivity to "being addressed" (510). Companies are comprised of human beings who are seeking to engage us as an audience with information that is relevant and meets our needs, wants, desires, and so on. For Tindale, the idea of receptivity on the part of the audience is of particular importance for argumentation. However, the rhetorical and persuasive nature of corporate communication and IMC also suggests an entry into argumentation.

Tindale (2013) notes that audience identity is of the utmost importance for any argument. He starts with an essential question of

> who the audience of any particular argumentative discourse is and proceed to the question of how an arguer can accommodate a composite audience comprised of different groups and individuals. A simple answer to the first question is that the audience is just whomever an arguer wishes to address by her or his argument. But this fails to appreciate the social character of much argumentation that circulates in spheres of influence rather than the limited domains of particular groups or individuals. (511)

Identity is, necessarily, complicated. Individual identity is made through a number of different characteristics, choices, and beliefs. For Tindale, because individual identity is complicated, understanding any audience is particularly difficult.

Tindale's contribution to argumentation finds ground in both corporate communication and IMC because practitioners must acknowledge the communication ethics implications that communication will have on audiences beyond traditional stakeholders. Corporate communication traditionally focused on communicating with "stakeholders and the general public" (Cornelissen 2017, 8). Cornelissen (2017) suggests, companies are "increasingly recognizing the need for an 'inclusive' and 'balanced' stakeholder management approach that involves actively communicating with *all* stakeholder groups on which the organization depends, and not just shareholders or customers" (8). Communication ethics helps to expand this approach particularly in drawing attention to the importance of communicating to others and making decisions that yield consequences for audiences and companies. A communication ethics stance to corporate communication involves making the choice to lessen the focus of any one individual person and to, instead, focus on building relationships with audiences through communication. Finding ethical ground becomes a necessity of a company's communication, especially in today's global society.

An understanding of communication ethics places emphasis on the common ethical ground upon which any company may stand. This announces a recognition of and openness to engage in ethical practices, accomplished through commitment to a shared emphasis on what is right (e.g., moral) for audiences. As Persuit (2013) posits, this calls for a consideration of message relevance. Corporate communication from an IMC perspective gives attention to audience beyond traditional stakeholders by starting with the audience and working backwards to think about how corporate communication works. Corporate communication is driven by the organization within (decisions made internally). Yet there must be a balance of understanding consumer voice (even if that means rejecting that voice for the sake of protecting organizational brand, identity, and reputation)—a company's corporate image. For example, a decision to participate (or not) in "greenwashing" evokes each of these factors. Greenwashing is "the term that describes companies' efforts to appear more environmentally sound than they are" (Pitrelli 2023). Today's consumers are looking for ways to be more responsible in changing their consumption practices, increasing the demand for companies to produce sustainable products and services (Pitrelli 2023). Companies *must* find balance between the consumer voice and their corporate image.

Cornelissen (2000) describes an image held by an audience "as a network of meanings stored in memory that range from holistic general impressions to very elaborate evaluations of objects" (120). Corporate image is an example of brand attitude strategy in which products have higher risk and the underlying motivation is *one* of the positive motives. Consequently, a consumer's awareness of a company or brand recognizes or recalls and constructs an image. Cornelissen further notes, "Meaning may be related to the tangible features of a corporate identity, but also consist of fleeting ephemeral perceptions that publics hold," such as a personal association of a company and a temporary feeling of about a decision the company makes to support or not support a social movement (120). Moreover, brand image involves audience perception, which ultimately impacts an audience member's view of the corporation (Cornelissen 2000). Together, these facets related to an image held by an audience form the interpretations of a human being and their involvement with a company and brand.

Current IMC practices and trends are shifting right now because the consumer is gaining more influence (becoming more involved). For companies and brands today, it all comes down to whether audiences will accept the corporate values of what the company or brand wants to adopt. Audiences will interpret and/or influence. With so much time dedicated to humanizing brands via the two-way communication espoused by IMC ideology, human beings are also branded, which subsequently evokes rhetorical and ethical implications. For example, on October 3, 2022, the Securities and Exchange Commission "announced charges against Kim Kardashian" for using her platform to promote a "crypto asset security" but neglecting to inform her followers that she was paid for the promotion (SEC 2022). In total, Kardashian was fined $1.26 million. Importantly, this example demonstrates a unique understanding of humans as brands. Because Kim Kardashian, arguably, is a brand herself, these legal troubles evoke challenge to her corporate values, a hallmark of corporate communication. Furthermore, that demonstrates the unique interplay between corporate communication and IMC or branding practices.

Kliatchko (2008), while focusing on IMC as a whole, recognizes the inherent importance of corporate communication in reconsidering IMC efforts. For Kliatchko, IMC as external communication depends upon the connection between "external audiences and the marketing activities directed to them with internal marketing efforts within the organization" (146). This unification allows for employees to understand the importance of considering audiences beyond stakeholders and prompts an organizational culture that is attentive to the needs and wants of consumers and audiences beyond traditional stakeholders. This move in organizational culture can, in the long term, provide stronger community relations and strong branding efforts to external audiences.

Patagonia's company founder demonstrated an awareness for the importance of finding ethical ground that simultaneously promotes organizational mission and rhetorical and ethical engagement of various audiences. In 2018, the company changed the company's purpose to "We're in business to save our home planet" (Chouinard 2022). On September 14, 2022, Patagonia's founder, Yvon Chouinard, followed through with this purpose and gave away his company. Chouinard wrote in letter, "Instead of 'going public,' you could say we're 'going purpose'" (Chouinard 2022). Chouinard (2022) notes,

100% of the company's voting stock transfers to the Patagonia Purpose Trust, created to protect the company's values; and 100% of the nonvoting stock had been given to the Holdfast Collective, a nonprofit dedicated to fighting the environmental crisis and defending nature.

Communication ethics assumes a responsibility to the other—people and places. In giving away the company, Chouinard recognizes his responsibility to the other—the environment—while also staying true to the company's purposes and, through the letter, reaches audiences beyond stakeholders.

Fundamentally, the Patagonia example demonstrates the importance of understanding corporate communication through an attentiveness to ethically responding to *all* audiences impacted by this company's business and communication practices. We maintain that this internal communication has significant implications for external communication, specifically branding and IMC. By understanding the importance of audience rhetorically and ethically in corporate communication, a company can essentially set the stage for strong branding practices that inevitably lead to brand loyalty and a strong IMC structure. The next section turns specifically to IMC, rhetorical audiences, and communication ethics to further unpack the implications of the intersection of these factors in this historical moment.

IMC AND ETHICS: UNDERSTANDING AUDIENCES BEYOND STAKEHOLDERS

This text assumes that corporate communication and IMC presuppose a need to involve the characteristics of persuasion and rhetoric into internal and external messaging by a company (e.g., marketing and advertising material). In a technological age, stakeholders are simply not the only audience that is impacted by brands. Today, more so than in the past, industry professionals must attend to communication and choice-making, recognizing that the consequences of choices expand beyond internal stakeholders. Despite societal pressures, industry professionals have an obligation to practice ethical decision-making, particularly in a cultural and historical moment in which public accountability is enforced by internal organizational actors *and* external public audiences. This call to action echoes a communication ethics perspective to lessen the focus of attention on the person and to refocus on building audience relationships.

Kliatchko (2008) notes, in his attempt to define IMC and its components in his work, that the concept of audience and stakeholder requires a rhetorical and ethical lens in the current communicative landscape. This is particularly important given that his work was published in 2008, and his contribution, arguably, is even more important today. His first pillar that he revisits is the idea of the "stakeholder," and in his description, he draws specific attention to the ethical dimensions of audience in the historical moment. Kliatchko notes that it is of the utmost importance to include rhetorical and ethical elements to IMC practices so as to accord "greater respect and value" to "stakeholders" as this "uphold[s] the dignity proper of the human person. Scholars have acknowledged the primordial role that moral values play in influencing consumer behavior" (146). Other scholars, like Kit Yarrow (2014), would echo this sentiment, articulating the central component of consumer psychology as central in a technological age.

Kliatchko cites authors like Bagozzi (1995) to further expand upon the moral considerations that factor into consumer behavior. This is essential in Kliatchko's (2008) redefinition of *content* in IMC, through which he notes that consumers are empowered to select their preferred media, and these preferences are significant in that consumers, in their selection, have power over the messaging they receive. Audiences have control. Kliatchko notes that this "participatory media" in the technological age rewrites the very definition of audience, whereby audiences are no longer passive, but active shapers of the media and messaging that they consume (148). The third concept that Kliatchko revisits, channel, specifically addresses the fact that "conventional media concepts, such as exposure, frequency, reach, and duplication are virtually obsolete" (151). The current communicative landscape is no longer cohesive. It is defined by a number of media choices, which subsequently suggests that consumer attention is harder to achieve although a company's message reaches more and more individuals (Bagozzi 1995). Kliatchko's revision to the IMC definition suggests a deeper attentiveness to ethics and to audience that responds to a changing technological environment.

Henninger, Alevizou, and Oates (2017) note that, in IMC, the "communication process should start with the consumer rather than the organization, to meet consumer needs more effectively" (670). The authors suggest that communication technologies and, more specifically social media, permit "dialogic communication" that assists in moving audiences to "consumer contact points" while simultaneously allowing for the communication to start with those particular audiences (670). Furthermore, the authors note how essential social media usage to facilitate dialogic communication can be in reaching any number of audiences, further demanding integration and consistency in messaging across a variety of channels. This, however, is a challenge in IMC in that increasing "fragmentation of media" means that "brands no longer have the power to control entirely what information is publicly available" (673). More importantly, as additional research suggests, that information can be both user-generated *and* reach audiences beyond traditional stakeholders.

For example, in 2019, British Airways relaunched their nonstop flight from Pittsburgh to London through the Pittsburgh International Airport. In order to market their return to Pittsburgh's airport, British Airways and VisitBritain placed an operating phone booth in a popular location for both tourists and Pittsburgh residents (CBS News 2019). Because of this geographic location's attentiveness to foot traffic, the location served as an ideal spot for the campaign. When pedestrians would answer the phone, they were asked a series of "quiz questions" and, simultaneously, had the opportunity to win a number of different prizes. If those who participated took a selfie next to the booth and used the hashtag #BALOVESPITTSBURGH, consumers could potentially win air travel to London, England (CBS News 2019). Though the phone booth is no longer there, the memory was impactful.

The example of British Airways is demonstrative of a number of key points in terms of audience, ethics, and rhetorical engagement of those audiences in a technological age. *CBS News* (2019) reported that the "Airport Authority estimates 50,000 people travel to London from this region [Pittsburgh] each year, and British Airways is betting a number of them will fly BA." Because British Airways recognized the potential market in the Pittsburgh region, they capitalized on an opportunity to draw attention to their company. More importantly, however, British Airways also saw an opportunity to speak to those audiences who were currently not directly within their target audience. The company generated a fun and engaging campaign that was appealing to audiences transcending stakeholders. Moreover, by integrating the social media component, they prompted word-of-mouth marketing with the potential to persuade other unknown audiences through the rhetorical appeals of the audiences themselves. Finally, British Airways also demonstrated an ethical lens turned toward marketing; they recognized a need, delivered persuasion that was sensitive to that need, and produced a product that matched their rhetoric.

Key and Czaplewski (2017) note that, in an increasingly "complex communicative landscape," any "audience can be difficult to target because the members are themselves a source of influence through their ability to make decisions and/or create policies" (326). In their work, Key and Czaplewski note that in any IMC campaign utilizing the proliferation of social media (and other) channels, there are audiences that extend beyond the traditional audience. They call these audiences "peripheral target audiences" (330), or "upstream" audiences (326). According to Gordon (2013), upstream audiences refers to "those who shape the structural and environmental conditions within society" (1529, qtd. in Key and Czaplewski 2017, 326). Drawn together, these two scholarly voices note that persuasion is not simply for one specific target audience. First, any target has the influence and power to influence other groups. Moreover, audiences must be attended to beyond a specific target audience, as other audiences hold influential power that can shape decisions from groups of people related to one's company.

In IMC practices, it is essential to understand that the rhetorical audience demands attention, comprising human beings. Responding to audience needs, wants, and characteristics makes for stronger messaging, particularly when tempered with an ethical understanding of the relationship among companies, organizations, and businesses in this technological environment. Companies increasingly have a responsibility to address the human component of communication and business strategies. As this work continues to consider the importance of audiences in this historical moment, we acknowledge that more and more companies are introducing technology and innovation into their branding activities, which we will consider in subsequent chapters. However, with technological advancements, there still exists a need for a human communication connection. Once acknowledged through a unification of corporate communication and IMC, moving to audiences beyond traditional stakeholders evokes a rhetorical and ethical turn that benefits businesses and audiences alike.

CORPORATE COMMUNICATION AND IMC: MOVING TO AUDIENCES BEYOND STAKEHOLDERS THROUGH RHETORIC AND COMMUNICATION ETHICS

This chapter frames the move to audiences beyond traditional stakeholders through a rhetorical and ethical lens. Devoid of rhetoric and communication ethics, corporate communication and IMC practices invite problematic culture and business practices that do not respond to the needs of both companies and their constituents. Kliatchko (2008) notes that "building and developing positive relationships, not only with the firm's external markets but also with its internal audience, is paramount, as it fosters in them a sense of loyalty and business ownership" (146). This is legitimately accomplished through uniting corporate communication and IMC with an eye toward ethically persuading audiences that extend beyond immediate publics and internal audiences.

In evaluating the motives of any given company, often we are faced with a dichotomous question: Do companies exist to help people or to make a profit? For most consumers, a company's bottom line does not factor into what audiences' factor into decision-making related to brand loyalty. Though the bottom line matters, a company's responsiveness to the human being in an audience matters most. Today, particularly for IMC, consumers and audiences are empowered to exert a communicative force that influences a company's decision-making. Specifically, communication technologies, such as social media, have permitted a two-way communication framework that IMC is responsive.

For example, in February 2023, M&M's, owned by Mars, announced it was taking an "indefinite pause" from using their "iconic spokescandies after updates to the characters 'broke the internet'" (Taylor 2023). In 2022, M&M's made changes to its spokescandies' appearances, giving them "a fresh new look" and "more nuanced personalities" (Taylor 2023). The changes created a backlash, a "melt in your hand" moment, by consumers and media outlets (most notably green M&M's boots) ("M&M'S® Concludes," 2023). This led the company to pause the use of the spokescandies and announce a "human spokesperson would be introduced" (O'Kane 2023). M&M's confirmed the pause in a public statement:

> America, let's talk. In the last year, we've made some changes to our beloved spokescandies. We weren't sure if anyone would notice. And we definitely didn't think it would break the internet. But now we get it—even a candy's shoes can be polarizing. Which was the last thing M&M's wanted since we're all about bring people together. Therefore, we have decided to take an indefinite pause from the spokescandies. In their place, we are proud to introduce a spokesperson America can agree on: the beloved Maya Rudolph. We are confident, Ms. Rudolph will champion the power of fun to create a world where everyone feels they belong. ("M&M's" 2023)

In the weeks following this statement, M&M's released a series of communications showing the spokescandies "pursuing other passions that reflect the characters' unique personalities, rooted in the M&M's purpose to bring people together to create a world where we all belong" ("M&M'S® Concludes" 2023). Then, Maya Rudolph made her debut in a Super Bowl ad as the new M&M's spokesperson, but M&M's included a twist with two additional pieces of content during the Big Game—one alluding to bringing back the spokescandies and the other a "'press-conference styled' commercial" announcing their return ("M&M'S® Concludes" 2023). The M&M's example is just one illustration of a company or brand using a two-way communication framework in its IMC, and, more specifically, how an empowered consumer's involvement is powerful, and with that involvement comes communicative impact that shapes brand loyalty and, often, brand equity.

In a complex communication environment, companies and brands are continually and increasingly working to meet the ethical demands of the consumer. If companies and brands do not deliver on the ethical demands of the consumer, a consumer relationship is unlikely (even not possible). Moreover, in this current historical moment, approaching a consumer relationship means to engage an audience both rhetorically and ethically. This moment calls for a return to Arnett and Arneson's (1999) concept of "dialogic civility," which requires having "respect for topics, others, multiple perspectives, and the given historical moment" (xii). When engaging in dialogic civility, a person takes into consideration the historical moment and the content and is mindful of the conversation no matter the difference between one another (xii). The same is true when companies and brands consider "the human behavior that drives most of our current understanding in today's business culture" and practices (Madsbjerg and Rasmussen 2014, 2). Such human behavior is not in seeing "people as predictable, rational decision makers," but, instead, emphasizes asking people "what they think and feel" (3). This requires companies and brands to move towards the recognition that they can have multiplicity in the audience engagement. Dialogic civility in relation to communication ethics, then, allows a company and brand to be who it is and the assurance that it can be different but still communicate together with others (e.g., audiences).

Dialogic civility simply recognizes that other views exist apart from a person's own unique or personal standpoint or perspective. In making this recognition, a person moves away from the private and into the public realm and is then engaging the other. Dialogic civility, then, discerns conversations taking place at a "public interpersonal level," though this level is of the non-intimate type (Arnett and Arneson 1999, xii). Dialogic civility, itself, is a relational praxis (theory-informed action) that exists when a genuine effort is made to make a conversation public and to understand the responsibility one has to the other to find a common ground (Arnett and Arneson 1999). This complex communication environment requires an openness to dialogic civility, rhetoric, and ethics insofar as human beings *must* recognize that two-way communication between companies and their audiences requires a sensitivity to the humans involved in the exchange. This work takes seriously these coordinates as we move to investigating the further implications of uniting corporate communication and IMC in a technological age. We turn to organizational culture to understand the embedded nature of these practices within our current historical moment.

Chapter 3

Organizational Culture at the Intersections of Corporate Communication and Integrated Marketing Communication

In June 2022, Indeed.com posted to its website an article by Daniel Humphries titled "Culture Is the DNA of the Company: An Interview with JetBlue's SVP of Talent, Rachel McCarthy." In it, Humphries (2017) noted that, in 2016, JetBlue was number twenty-one on Indeed's "Best Companies to Work For" list, and, in 2017, the company had reached the number three spot. In speaking with JetBlue employees, they routinely pointed to *culture* as being a primary reason that employees loved the company that they worked for. Quoting Rachel McCarthy, the senior vice president of talent and learning at JetBlue, Humphries (2017) writes that "JetBlue was founded on 'bringing humanity back to air travel,' says McCarthy." Citing its five core values ("safety, caring, integrity, passion, and fun"), McCarthy notes that JetBlue utilizes these values in structuring *all* of its communication—with both external and internal audiences alike. For McCarthy, "the culture is the DNA of the company, what fuels us. It's not one thing, it's woven through a number of things" (Humphries 2017). Culture, then, is demonstrative of organizational and corporate attitudes integrated between and among various audiences beyond traditional stakeholders.

Edward Schein and Peter Schein (2016) suggest that corporate cultures are *"macro* cultures" in that they may possess "corporate cultures in spite of the obvious presence of many diverse subcultures within the larger organization" (13). Importantly, culture acts as an overarching guide to learning and understanding organizational history, behavior, assumptions, and communication. At the macro level, and as echoed by McCarthy's statements, culture can act as organizational structure, guiding the behaviors of all levels of employees and all groups of stakeholders. This chapter maintains that broad organizational culture, under this framework, acts as a structural framework that guides communication practices, including corporate communication and IMC, and should be attended to when engaging with audiences beyond traditional stakeholders.

This chapter continues with an overview of organizational communication and organizational culture in the communication literature, a discussion of organizational culture's impact on corporate communication, a review of IMC and holistic approaches to culture, and implications for understanding the impact of organizational culture on the practices of corporate communication and IMC. Organizational culture in today's historical moment *should* filter through all communication strategies and initiatives. Today, internal and external stakeholders and audiences are receiving messaging *together*, and are impacted by companies' communication and action in the public sphere. According to Hatch and Schultz (1997), in past moments, companies separated the internal and external communication, businesses, and strategies within their culture because internal and external audiences were, often, kept apart (356). This is no longer the communicative landscape that brands and their consumers inhabit. Understanding the interplay between organizational communication, organizational culture, and strategic communication offers an entrance for companies to meet the historical moment. We begin with an overview of organizational communication and culture to contextualize the needs of this historical moment.

ORGANIZATIONAL COMMUNICATION AND CULTURE: AN OVERVIEW

Understanding the concept of a company or a brand in this current historical moment is not an isolated objective analysis but, rather, characterized by human interpretation *and* communication in both the marketplace and in culture. Charles Perrow (2015) argued that an organization's "purpose" is collective, meaning that companies, brands, and *all* of their audiences find a common center through that purpose, invoking collective participation (76). As this common purpose is even more prevalent in the current climate of the public sphere, we turn to an overview of organizational communication, as its foundations provide an essential and formative scholarly inquiry with impacts for the *practices* of corporate communication and IMC.

The development of the area of organizational communication has historically been dominated by paradigmatic theories that contextualize organizations as being created by communication practices. In both theory and practice, organizational communication is the foundation for recognizing the centrality of communication in the actual activity of organizing in business practices (Putnam and Mumby 2013, 4). At the heart of organizational communication, the emphasis upon communicative practices creates not only a company but also its culture. In our current historical moment, globalization, emerging technologies, and economic conditions have shifted traditional distinctions between public and private lives (Arendt 1958). Because of this, organizational life continually shifts to reflect both public considerations and personal value. For example, in April 2022, as the constraints of the Covid-19 pandemic were beginning to lessen, approximately 4.4 million American workers resigned from their jobs, which was an even smaller number than March of that same year (Kaplan and Hoff 2022). Kaplan and Hoff report that April 2022 was the eleventh consecutive month that saw over four million Americans leave their jobs. Pew Research Center reported that this "Great Resignation," beginning in 2021, occurred for a number of reasons. Of those who left their job in 2021, 63% of people reported low pay, 63% reported lack of upward mobility, and 57% reported feeling unappreciated and "disrespected" (Parker and Menasce 2022). In addition, 48% reported not having adequate childcare, 45% reported lack of flexibility in working hours, and 43% lamented the lack of benefits, including "paid time off" (Parker and Menasce 2022). Concepts such as flexibility, mobility, and meaningful work are lacking in conversations centered upon work-life balance, and should be addressed in organizational culture to continue to positively impact organizational life.

Work-life balance, organizational culture, and communication create an interplay of ethical considerations that further enhance our understanding of the current climate today. As Ronald C. Arnett (2005) points out in *Dialogic Confessions*, confession used in the marketplace (e.g., companies) is encompassed by four major human institutions to assist in the fragile absolute and to overcome moral crisis. The human institutions require constant effort to influence all dimensions in life without losing respect for their individual autonomy; special places for people to congregate within (Arnett 2005). One of the human institutions dimensions is *culture* (Arnett 2005). The culture of a company is a coordinate that announces a commitment to moral engagement in this historical moment. Lack of moral engagement can be devastating to company culture. As of the writing of this book, technology and digital companies were routinely announcing employee layoffs. According to a *Wall Street Journal* article, Google, Microsoft, Amazon, and other tech companies laid off more than 70,000 employees in 2022 (Capoot and Pitt 2023). While layoffs in companies are sometimes necessary, the communication practices used to deliver the news are not always appropriate. For example, many technology companies are choosing to inform workers they were being laid off by email. A *New York Times* article addresses how the trend in email layoff notifications dehumanizes workers, and ultimately treats "employees like disposable units who can simply be unsubscribed" (Spiers 2023). For companies delivering bad news to employees, such as layoffs, a commitment to moral engagement demonstrates a responsibility to the other (the employee) beyond the self (the company). This is guided by organizational culture and communication.

Because of the embedded nature of organizational communication and, more specifically, organizational life, its impact on corporate communication and IMC cannot go unnoticed. As Daniel Coyle (2018) discusses in *The Culture Code*, "culture is a set of living relationships working toward a shared goal. It's not something you are. It's something you do" (xx). Culture extends beyond communication; it is fundamentally communication *in* action, reflecting value and standpoint. Because culture reflects so much of organizational life, all relationships are impacted, including those with audiences beyond traditional stakeholders. Understanding organizational culture begins to offer a structural framework for understanding its role in this work's larger conversation.

Organizational culture is a central tenet in the organizational communication literature, and has been defined by many scholars and industry professionals. Culture is, fundamentally, communicative in nature (Schein and Schein 2016). Culture is *observable*, and temporally exists through past participation and present action (6). This process occurs through the collective and communicative effort that individuals make in the participation in a "pattern or system of beliefs, values, and behavioral norms that come to be taken for granted as basic assumptions and eventually drop out of awareness" (6). Culture acts as formative for organizational life in that it offers communicative significance in the everyday behaviors of the individuals that comprise the organization (6). Moreover, in organizational life, these everyday behaviors exist as both an *external* form of communication (this is who we are) and *internal* (this is who we understand ourselves to be).

For the practices of corporate communication and IMC, this distinction is essential. Culture begins internally in an organization; however, it is also a product of external communication as it frames the ways in which companies and brands communicate about identity and values (Schein and Schein 2016, 7). Even further, successful companies in the public sphere that boast both "successful performance and effective learning" are careful to ensure that audiences within and outside of the organization are coherently connected with one another (8). This integration of culture at the external and internal level is a central tenet of IMC branding practices today; understanding *who* a company is, is a key feature in decision-making by audiences and should factor into those communication practices.

In today's global society, organizational culture must also be attentive to the intercultural communication necessary to attend to the various cultures that come together within the company. This dynamic is essential and one that corporate communication and IMC practices *must* also be attentive to. Within the scope of this project, we focus upon organizational culture understood as the collective members of an organization, involving "sense-making" (Hatch and Schultz 1997, 360), which is "founded on a broad-based history that realized in the material aspects (or artifacts) of the organization (e.g., its name, products, buildings, logos and other symbols, including its top managers)" (359). This definition moves the understanding of organizational culture to acknowledge both corporate communication and IMC practices. Beginning with corporate communication, we frame the implications of organizational culture on moving to audiences beyond traditional stakeholders.

CORPORATE COMMUNICATION AND CULTURE: BEGINNING WITH INTERNAL AUDIENCES

More recently, there has been an increased level of conversation happening globally around workplace culture (i.e., what it is, why it matters, how to achieve it). As of the writing of this book, the globe is adjusting to a "new normal" due to the Covid-19 pandemic. Subsequently, companies are faced with questions around on-site/remote/hybrid work options. For some companies, the answer to such questions are clear, but for others, answers to these questions are nebulous, leaving companies with challenging moral decision-making. In this section, we focus on how companies use internal communication (e.g., employee relations) to establish workplace culture and how it influences internal practices like purpose, mission, and vision.

Frank and Brownell (1989) define internal communication as "the communications transitions between individuals and/or groups at various levels and in different areas of specialization that are intended to design and redesign organizations, to implement design, and to co-ordinate day-to-day activities" (5–6). The purpose of internal communication is to provide effective communication at and between all levels of an organization. Argenti (1996) refers to internal communication as a subfunction of corporate communication, noting that as companies continue to focus on "a happy workforce with changing values and different demographics, they have necessarily had to think more seriously about how they communicate with employees through what is often referred to as internal communications" (80). A company must think strategically about how it communicates with its employees through internal communication, and strong communication is a necessity to maintain trust and boost morale.

Every year, the international public relations firm Edelman releases the Edelman Trust Barometer. Number one on the 2022 Edelman Trust

Barometer's "The Trust 10" is "distrust is now society's default emotion" ("Edelman Trust 10" 2022). According to the study, "nearly 6 in 10 say their default tendency is to distrust something until they see evidence it is trustworthy" ("Edelman Trust 10" 2022). This study, importantly, notes that any lack of trust impedes the ability for companies to communicate with their many audiences and stakeholders. This, in turn, creates significant challenges for operations in the marketplace. Companies across the globe are faced with monitoring trust levels.

An example of internal communication and the impact it can have on building and maintaining trust with employees can be seen with Uber. Uber, the tech giant, made headlines in July 2022 when leaked "Uber files" exposed how Uber was capitalizing on violence against drivers under then-CEO Travis Kalanick (Mueller 2022). The leaked files revealed attempts to lobby politicians, break laws, and exploit violence against its drivers (Davies and Goodley 2022). In a statement, Uber acknowledged "mistakes" were made under Kalanick and "it's exactly why Uber hired a new CEO, Dara Khosrowshahi, who was tasked with transforming every aspect of how Uber operates" (Davies and Goodley 2022). The leaked files reveal the dark side of a company and how much employee trust, just like in any interpersonal relationship, can be solid one day and the very next be damaged with only the possibility for repair. For companies, lack of trust can become an organizational moral crisis and necessitate an overhaul in workplace culture.

Demonstrating empathy and compassion is crucial to helping human beings to recognize that others in the conversation and in the culture of that specific place (company) bring equally important values and/or ideas. Communication expressed in such a way that people are affirming their own work and it is fueled by their concern for others (e.g., co-workers). In this way, empathy and compassion deal with lived experiences among not only internal audiences but external ones as well. Organizational culture is driven by recreation of tenets such as the mission, purpose, and vision of companies, which is then promoted through its corporate communication and IMC to audiences beyond traditional stakeholders.

Deal and Kennedy (2000) discuss the importance of having a solid company culture and articulate their view that strong communication and strong values reveal better companies. Companies with strong cultures, of course, do not all have the same values, but demonstrate a commitment to values through their communicative actions. The biggest quality issue in any company is the people. Employees are the most responsible, and communication is intensely important to how any company can function. For example, one indicator of a strong culture is to ask the question: What is the nature of the turnover in the company? How a company practices culture and communicates culture matters. Strong organizational cultures promote from within, and use corporate communication to create cultural meaning in communication exchanges within companies. This idea creates a corporate culture that invites "dialogic civility," because companies essentially seek to keep the conversation going between human beings (Arnett and Arneson 1999, xii).

According to Johnstone (1981), the "humanist commitment" in organizational communication centered upon an understanding that our humanness is brought into all aspects of life. Johnstone notes that "the humanist commitment demands a dedication to nurturing and treasuring those characteristics in ourselves and each other that underlie our capacity for bringing quality into our lives" (188). Johnstone's understanding of the humanist commitment is reflected in the mission, purpose, and vision of companies which allows their unique corporate cultures to thrive. If a company is striving to be a standard-bearer (an expert) in its respective industry, then it must demonstrate a commitment to its mission, purpose, and vision through its communicative actions.

The mission, purpose, and vision of companies are grounded in the narrative of the organization. An example is illustrated by Southwest Airlines. With the innovative ideas of Rollin King and Herb Kelleher, Southwest Airlines started its service on June 18, 1971. King and Kelleher "began with one simple notion: If you get your passengers to their destinations when they want to get there, on time, at the lowest possible fares, and make darn sure they have a good time doing it, people will fly your airline" (*Book Flights* 2022). Southwest faced adversity with being a small domestic airline competing with larger companies, but in the end, King and Kelleher were right. Today, Southwest has more than 4,000 flights a day, making the company the largest carrier of domestic passengers in the United States (*Book Flights* 2022). Southwest offers consistently cheap fares and innovative customer benefits, such as a frequent flyer program that emphasizes number of trips taken rather than miles flown. Southwest was also the first airline to introduce senior discounts, fun fares, companion fares, and an online fare alert service direct to customers' computers (DING!) (*Book Flights* 2022). Southwest has remained a leader within the airline industry because it understands that the most important keys to success are satisfied customers and, perhaps more importantly, happy employees.

The narrative of Southwest Airlines can be looked at through its mission, purpose, and vision statements. The Southwest mission is "dedication to the highest quality of Customer Service delivered with a sense of warmth, friendliness, individual pride, and Company Spirit"; its purpose is to "connect people to what's important in their lives through friendly, reliable, and low-cost air travel"; and its vision is "to become the world's most loved, most flown, and most profitable airline (*Book Flights* 2022). Southwest's mission, purpose, and vision statements provide a guiding story for the company and give a blueprint for future action.

Some of Southwest's unique business strategies and practices include pricing structure, ticketless travel, and a boarding process with no seat assignments. From 1989, Southwest has remained a low-fare leader. Southwest developed the "ticketless" travel option, strengthening customer satisfaction tremendously. "Ticketless" flights are far more flexible than ticketed flights because in the event that the flight is cancelled or the customer cannot make it to the flight, there will be a credit made in the purchaser's name that can be used as funds for a flight for the purchaser or it can be used to issue a ticket to whomever the purchaser decides to give the tickets out to, for up to a year. Southwest was also an innovator in the no-seat-assignment boarding process. With this process, passengers do not have to fear the burden of sitting uncomfortably with three people in one row on a plane that only contains a few numbers of passengers (*Book Flights* 2022).

Since Kelleher founded Southwest, he enforced a way of business operations that is like no other airline, providing a kind of dialogic civility that has been unmatched by any other company in its field. Today, the airline continues to be prosperous while following the mission, purpose, and vision set by its founder (*Book Flights* 2022). Southwest is known for its employee satisfaction; these professional relationships lead to superb problem-solving techniques, training and hiring of new employees, and customer satisfaction. Many have tried to imitate the way Southwest runs as a business, but none have come close to the kind of success Kelleher's leadership and guidance have achieved. Southwest's deep tradition of customer care and nurturing of employees has propelled its position as an industry leader.

Community in companies depends on sacred passion and commitment. Jim Collins (2005), in *Good to Great and the Social Sectors*, refers to great companies as those who "focused on getting and hanging on to the right people in the first place those who are productively neurotic, those who are *self-motivated* and *self-disciplined*, those who wake up every day, compulsively driven to do the best they can because it is simply part of their DNA" (15). Finding the right people matters. Finding people who choose what matters is also a necessity in today's global society. This, however, is often put aside by companies in order to meet a bottom line. In *Firms of Endearment*, Sisodia, Wolfe, and Sheth (2007) remind us that "it's not share of wallet . . . it's share of heart" (1). This is what fosters a sense of *common good* within a company.

In today's complex global society, it takes a company with a strong sense of community to guard the common good. The pressures to show a profit are continually heightening, even for the social sector. This historical moment requires business acumen as a demonstrator of the right to exist. The soul of a company is communicated through its mission, purpose, and vision. This does not mean that making a profit should be put by the wayside. It would be impractical to think that a company could sustain itself on something like care for the community, alone. Thus, what is emerging today suggests that passion must always be met and matched by social business practices.

Focusing on audiences and making a profit are not mutually exclusive. In fact, suitability necessitates financial attentiveness, even gain. The key is not to place profit as the primary point of concern. In the spirit of Aristotelian economic thought, companies must identify their role and fulfill that role— the profit will then follow (Meikle 1997). Profitability fits in this framework because companies gain to broaden their reach and influence the other, and subsequently support the existence of the company. It is important for a company to stay mission driven and not become a commercial venture because loving profit in the wrong way leads a company to lose its soul.

The heart of a company is its commitment to its people. The center of this commitment is its mission. An organization's mission rests in what Bellah et al. (2008) refer to as "habits of the heart" (37). The term "habits of the heart" was first coined by Alexis de Tocqueville (1835) in *Democracy of America*, in which he "speaks of mores somewhat loosely, defining them variously as 'habits of the heart'; notions, opinions and ideas that 'shape mental habits'; and 'the sum of moral and intellectual dispositions of men in society'" (Bellah et al. 2008, 37). A company's "habits of the heart" are illustrated practically as its mission. Mission statements are often developed based on a company's values, attitudes, and beliefs, or its "habits of the heart." Collins (2005) posits, building a strong reputation matters for companies. Audiences *must* "believe not only in your mission, but your capacity to deliver on that mission" (25). In practical terms, "habits of the heart" can be understood as the nonnegotiables of a company.

A company lives out its mission working within the spirit of what Emmanuel Kant (1892) refers to as an "enlarged mentality." This level of engagement presupposes the importance of reflecting on the values, attitudes, and beliefs of the self and the other, seeking common ground that establishes a sacred space for building and enhancing the lives of those embodied in the mission. No doubt, it is value that makes a "pragmatic difference in one's life and in one's community" (Fisher 1989, 111). Human values offer and create character; however, common values are a minimal set of agreements that announce a community's (e.g., a company's) willingness to work together (Bok 1995). A minimal set of values makes possible communal growth (even in conflict), and communicates concern for the larger community—for the company.

Shared growth depends on human beings engaging and vetting ideas for real use in the company. This is a *nonnegotiable* for companies, and, if lacking, will impact the organizational culture and, more specifically, employee engagement. The "quiet quitting" trend in the workplace provides a good example. Quiet quitting is coined as "an approach to work in which individuals meet the minimum requirements of their job description but nothing more—no discretionary effort, no going above and beyond" (Harter 2022). According to Gallup (2022) research, "'quiet quitters' make up at least 50% of the U.S. workforce." For Gallup, "quiet quitters" is not a new term, but rather fits into its category of people who are "not engaged" at work (Harter 2022). Employee engagement is an important facet for any company and maintaining a strong organizational culture. Gallup (2022) research findings point to "poor management practices" (e.g., communication) as the contributor to quiet quitting and, therefore, employees who are not engaged at work. Accordingly, the role of organizational culture is clear, committed action toward the other (e.g., people and places).

Companies can offer signs of hope when a sense of community in society has been disrupted by an unforeseen event. It is the responsibility of the company to do what is best for its community (its audiences) and not for the company (the self). It is the place that fills the void, providing hope in the sense of an unfettered time, allowing a company to position itself favorably in the minds of audiences beyond traditional stakeholders. For example, in 1982, Johnson and Johnson voluntarily recalled their Tylenol product after someone had "tampered with capsules of Extra-Strength Tylenol, turning them lethal with potassium cyanide" and killing several people (Haberman 2018). Widely acknowledged as responsible action, this case is still not forgotten. In 2022, authorities continue to investigate this case, and are actively seeking to bring justice to the person responsible for the loss of life (NBC Chicago 2022). Importantly, NBC Chicago (2022) reports that "in addition to sparking a panic across the Chicago area and the U.S., the murders forever changed the way we consume medicine, prompting the introduction of tamper-evident pill containers." Essentially, in response to this unforeseen crisis, Johnson and Johnson responded to protect its audience, issued strategic and helpful communication, and took communicative action to prevent something like this ever occurring again.

The workplace today is different, and companies *must* consider why and how their corporate communication aligns with their organizational culture as well as what additional communicative practices will help shape their future. As Qin et al. (2022) note, "purpose, mission and vision statements are all important corporate components that companies use to communicate their values and beliefs" (426). Companies can strengthen relationships with audiences by communicating through corporate communication how their values and beliefs are practiced in their daily business operations.

Today audiences expect the norm (not deviation from) to participate in the conversations associated with companies. Through an attentiveness to organizational culture, company corporate communication is enhanced in a manner that focuses upon relationships with audiences extending beyond traditional stakeholders. Furthermore, in today's historical moment, ensuring strong corporate values can enhance and strengthen branding practices. In moving to IMC, we consider the impact of corporate values on organizational life and success with audiences.

IMC: A CORPORATE PHILOSOPHY OF ORGANIZATIONAL CULTURE

In the beginning of their 1997 article, Hatch and Schultz note that "one of the primary challenges faced by contemporary organizations stems from the breakdown of the boundary between their internal and external aspects" (356). For the authors, organizational identity *is* a subset of organizational culture, and identity is specific to the components of a company that comprise its image, reputation, and overall position in the market. That image is defined by these authors as a "holistic and vivid impression held by an individual or a particular group towards an organization and is a result of sensemaking by the group *and* communication by the organization of a fabricated and projected picture of itself" (359). Though a direct result of marketing efforts, naturally, this is also a direct result of the interplay between internal and external audiences, moving this beyond simply stakeholders (Hatch and Schultz 1997). We argue that organizational culture, identity, and image must be fostered amongst *all* audiences so as to carry forth the basic tenets of IMC and branding. Integrating messaging to project brand awareness and position is necessary each and every single time a consumer interacts with that brand.

This cannot be accomplished by adopting this philosophy only in an IMC, advertising, or marketing department. Rather, a company or brand must acknowledge the centrality of the unification of its corporate communication practices with its IMC practices. IMC has been practiced and researched under a number of names and in a number of iterations. Iglesias, Sauquet, and Montaña (2011) refer to "relationship marketing" as "emphasi[zing] the importance of establishing and maintaining relationships between customers and buyers, in comparison to the transactional orientation of the classical marketing paradigm" (632). The emphasis upon relationships is an essential function of IMC and, as Iglesias, Sauquet, and Montaña (2011) articulate, must develop *from* a culture that is in support of these communicative measures. Many authors have argued and emphasized that specific *types* of cultures better support IMC efforts (e.g., Porcu et al. 2020), and this demonstrates how essential culture is to the successful implementation of IMC for companies and brands.

Robyn Blakeman (2018) notes that "IMC fails when it is seen as just another communication effort rather than a corporate philosophy expressed both inside and out" (6). IMC as a corporate practice reflects a strategic understanding of the new social and cultural landscape that has shifted consumer expectations within branding and stakeholder relationships with companies. For Blakeman, IMC must be enacted as a corporate philosophy in that consumers form relationships with brands at all interaction points with companies. As such, IMC is not simply a practice but must be a part of organizational culture in order to achieve its goals of strengthened consumer relationships as well as strong brand positioning in the marketplace.

For example, Patagonia boasts strong communication strategies that consistently align with its corporate communication. Because of that, the company's IMC efforts are significantly enhanced. The company notes immediately on its website that it has "transitioned away from allowing permanent branding or logos to our gear" (Patagonia n.d.). For Patagonia, this decision was made based exclusively on corporate values. The company's "business" is "to save our home planet" (Patagonia n.d.). Because of that, adding permanent branding on its clothing reduces its lifespan. The website reads: "When we made this decision, we accepted that it might cost us some business. But we hope you'll see this shift for what it is: another of our ongoing efforts to support a healthy planet—and a call to action" (Patagonia n.d.). Patagonia then issued the "call to action," calling for audiences who are hoping to purchase its gear with the knowledge that the purchaser is "making a statement about your own commitment to sustainability" (Patagonia n.d.). Though the effort is to remove explicit branding on its clothing, this example of IMC offers a unique glimpse into the power of successful integration of a company's internal and external communication. Furthermore, what is clear is that branding as a whole, when practiced as a corporate philosophy, clearly announces value to audiences beyond traditional stakeholders that carries with it an appeal to additional audiences.

Adopting IMC as a corporate philosophy, according to Blakeman (2018), ensures the process of integration, which Schultz and Shultz (2004) determine to be a marketing need in this current historical moment. As they note, "over the years, it has become clear that customers relate to brands, not to the various forms of marketing or marketing communication" (xvii). The humanizing of the brand, particularly in the 2020s, has shifted into an emphasis on both consumer and brand alike. In their article, "An Inside-Out Approach to

Integrated Marketing Communication: An International Analysis," Kerr et al. (2008) suggest that integration in advertising and marketing is not a new phenomenon, but the integration was particularly difficult to implement with increasingly siloed practices of advertising and then marketing. .

Kit Yarrow (2014) noted that the new consumer expects a certain degree of involvement with branding and marketing. She notes that "today, people are willing to be involved in every aspect of that process—from what's made, to how it's produced, to where it's sold. They are willing to engage in promoting and even selling it themselves" (153). As new consumer expectations take hold of the marketplace, the high level of expectations from consumers pushes marketing into the very fibers of organizational life and culture. More specifically, IMC must come to be seen as a core component of organizational culture.

Porcu et al. (2017) comment that IMC has gained in traction in both academia and in the marketplace *because* of the "dynamic technological environment that great affects the marketing and corporate communication processes" (121). While we will address technology in a separate chapter, this essential point is of the utmost importance in the context of organizational culture. Specifically, these authors define IMC through a number of scholars, but ultimately determine the practice to be a company-wide solution to involving all components of an organization in the promotion of brand values, mission, vision, and so on (124). Porcu et al. (2017) note that because "IMC involves the entire organization, the most critical issue is how it should be organized; therefore, the organizational system elements are expected to greatly affect integration" (123). Moreover, the authors point to *culture* as particularly impactful. Essentially, the history of IMC, current definitions, and current practices all suggest that, because IMC involves an entire company, it is impacted by organizational culture in important ways. Depending upon leadership style, organizational climate, and communication practices, IMC as an approach is responsive to the framing that is done by cultural guidelines and rules.

Schein and Schein (2016) maintain that "groups do not exist in isolation. To get something done requires some kind of action in the various environments in which the group is embedded" (8). When we move beyond stakeholders to audiences, this note on organizational culture carries with it significant ramifications for both branding and IMC. Hatch and Schultz (1997) contend that "when we express organizational identity we use our cultural artefacts symbolically to present an image that will be interpreted by others" (360). For the authors, identity as a function of organizational culture provides the foundational factors that create image and reputation, and subsequently create a foundation for communication strategies (361). They depend upon one another to interact with audiences at all levels.

According to Turner and Spencer (1994), culture promotes clarity for internal audiences on organizational value and character, emphasizing participation and dedication to the organization in meaningful ways. Integrating the principles of marketing and reviewing the, then, current literature, the authors suggest that "when organizational culture is comprised of organizational-wide shared meaning, values, and beliefs placing the customer at the center of the decision-making process, the attainment of long-term corporate goals and objectives will be facilitated" (112). In IMC, placing the consumer at the center is not only exceedingly important, but also an essential function of this strategic communication discipline that takes seriously the notion of two-way communication between brand and consumer. This move, which Harris (1998) notes coincided with an evolving emphasis on attending to issues of culture, must holistically acknowledge the needs and expectations of consumers in this historical moment.

Porcu et al. (2020) argue that IMC, to be successful in its goals of relationship building, should be inherent within the organizational structure itself "to enable it to achieve a clear orientation toward all its stakeholders, both internal (employees) and external (shareholders, suppliers, customers, distributors, and so on)" (436). In defining IMC, the authors emphasize routinely that strong implementation of IMC involves the entirety of a business. One of the key elements to defining IMC, for the authors, is "organizational alignment," which they define through a literature review as entire organizational participation, at all levels, with IMC philosophies (436–437). The significance of their work is in the suggestion that IMC, definitionally, requires organizational culture to adopt this strategic communication plan both top-down and bottom-up. Moreover, organizational culture *feeds* IMC practices. The symbols associated with culture, the mission statements that structure core values, and the beliefs and values embedded within the organization should ultimately be reflected in messaging and persuasive strategies.

Without question, organizational culture is a necessary element of any brand that wishes to engage audiences that extend beyond traditional stakeholders. More importantly, organizational culture allows for the successful implementation of IMC, strengthening branding practices in an era that relies upon branding as a primary communicative vehicle to engaging audiences. With a look toward both internal and external communication, organizational culture influences all elements of organizational communication and, therefore, has significant impacts on all audiences that are confronted with organizational messaging. In examining culture, understanding the interplay of corporate communication and IMC is essential to engaging with audiences beyond stakeholders today.

UNITING CORPORATE COMMUNICATION
AND IMC IN ORGANIZATIONAL CULTURE

Understanding organizational culture has significant implications for understanding the strategic importance of corporate communication and IMC in today's historical moment and global public sphere. When done well, aligning corporate values and corporate communication with IMC and branding efforts presents a holistic image of the organization to a number of audiences extending beyond traditional stakeholders, which is a valuable communicative activity in this moment. However, when this is not done well, organizational problems emerge that have detrimental effects on the brand *and* corporate bottom line.

For example, Facebook (now under the parent company of Meta) has faced scrutiny for not upholding corporate values, which significantly impacts its brand as a whole. In 2021, Frances Haugen, a former data scientist at Facebook, reported Facebook "harms children, sows division, and undermines democracy in pursuit of breakneck growth and 'astronomical profits'" (Allyn 2021). Haugen said Facebook broke the law, and her lawyers filed multiple complaints with the Securities and Exchange Commission on Facebook's public statements (Allyn 2021). While Haugen received global attention as the Facebook whistleblower, Facebook needed to address its illegal (and unethical) business activity. In a post, Facebook CEO Mark Zuckerberg wrote, "We care deeply about issues like safety, well-being and mental health" (Zuckerberg 2021). He said he is "particularly focused on the questions raised about our work with kids . . . and, it's very important to me that everything we build is safe and good for kids" (Zuckerberg 2021). Zuckerberg concluded the post with "I think about the real impact we have on the world—the people who can now stay in touch with their loved ones, create opportunities to support themselves, and find community" (Zuckerberg 2021). As Persuit (2013) notes, "a rhetorical approach to social media and IMC encourages phronesis [practical wisdom] developed by engaging in deliberation and reasoned choice" (106). The same is true for the use of corporate communication and IMC during organizational crisis. In the case of Facebook, the internal communications did not match what was being expressed externally to audiences, causing audiences to question Facebook's values and beliefs.

While we have yet to see, as of the writing of this book, the implications behind this example, Meta faces challenges that present implications for the understanding of audiences beyond traditional stakeholders. While the alignment between corporate communication and IMC is a necessary practice, providing messaging that contradicts values with branding efforts *and* communicative action draws the attention of *all* audiences, regardless of whether or not those audiences act as traditional stakeholders. Strengthening organizational culture and living that culture both internally and externally carry with them opportunities for continued growth and brand loyalty in today's marketplace that is impacted by communication technologies. As the next chapter will detail, the technological age has, without question, drawn the attention of audiences to this alignment with more scrutiny than ever before.

Chapter 4

Corporate Communication and Integrated Marketing Communication in a Technological Age

On May 10, 2019, *Forbes Magazine* published an article written by Braze, a platform that connects brands with stakeholders, titled "How 'Human' Is Your Brand?" The article, a paid program piece, notes, "We're in the age of the consumer. Brands need to be customer-first. Customer-centric. Customer-*obsessed*" (Braze 2019). This shift to "customer-centric" rhetoric is not *just* a rhetorical move but, rather, a reflection of needed strategic communication that responds to our technological age (Braze 2019). Braze is responsible for a service known as the Braze Brand Humanity Index, which intentionally emphasizes the need to generate *real human connections* between brand and customer. This article emphasizes one key point important to emphasize in the move to engaging audiences beyond stakeholders in a technological age. Specifically, strong branding practices are emotional and human. However, "we're also in the midst of a digital revolution, a time when there are more devices than human beings on the planet. So we have to be more human, but achieving that end means leveraging technology" (Braze 2019). In a digital age, the move to be more human means to understand the ways in which humans communicate and build relationships.

Corporate communication and IMC are two strategic communication functions that move companies to consider audiences beyond their immediate stakeholders, and in this new digital age, marked by an increase in demand upon companies and brands to connect with humans, a greater emphasis is placed upon understanding the ways in which *consumers* communicate. This chapter begins with a basic assumption: engaging with audiences *beyond* traditional stakeholders is an essential need in business and marketing communication and a function of organizational life *because* of the influx of communication technologies. Companies have routinely been responsible to audiences beyond immediate stakeholders; the influx of communication technologies has made this responsibility ever present and an essential component of all corporate communication strategies and branding functions.

This chapter includes a brief overview of definitions of media ecology as a philosophical area of study, a description of corporate communication in a digital age, a description of integrated marketing communication in a digital age, and major implications for business and marketing communication in our current historical moment. Importantly, companies and brands are featured in the forefront of human communication in popular culture and the public sphere. Social media, in particular, has altered the communicative landscape and, with it, expectations for communication between and among human beings and brands. In a technological age, companies are called to respond to the changing communication expectations but, also, to recognize the influx of audiences that are impacted by their messaging in today's public sphere. By considering the study of media ecology in connection to corporate communication and IMC, this chapter addresses those expectations and considers the impacts upon audiences.

MEDIA ECOLOGY: A COMMUNICATION PERSPECTIVE ON TECHNOLOGY AND THE MARKETPLACE

We begin with a brief introductory overview of the area of inquiry known as "media ecology" in order to situate corporate communication and IMC in a technological age. This field of academic inquiry has been founded and shaped by major thinkers such as Marshall McLuhan, Harold Innis, Walter Ong, Neil Postman, Lewis Mumford, Jacques Ellul, Eric Havelock, and Lance Strate, among others (Strate 2019). Significantly, these major thinkers' oeuvre of work provides a historical overview of the development of thought and tracing of media throughout all of the history of civilization to track how media forms and impacts our environments and communicative life.

According to Lance Strate, media ecology is "the study of media environments, the idea that technology and techniques, modes of information and codes of communication, play a leading role in human affairs" (Strate 2019). In all of human communication, the environment impacts and shapes the expectations for the "rules" of engaging with others. Neil Postman suggests that media ecology considers how "media of communication affect human perception, understanding, feeling, and value; and how our interaction with media facilitates or impedes our chances of survival" (Postman 1970, qtd. in Strate 2019). Beyond the rules of engaging with others (immediacy, language, etc.), communication technologies also reflect cultural values, beliefs, and assumptions. The founders of media ecology consider the impacts of media on the various environments in which media shapes human discourse and interaction.

Neil Postman pushes against the idea that communication technologies are neutral additions to our communicative and cultural environment (Postman 2000, 11). Technology cannot be neutral, says Postman, because it changes the ways in which human beings approach the world and approach one another. Technology changes our human environments. To further distinguish his position on communication technologies, Postman defines both media and ecology to demonstrate their significant impacts on human culture and understanding (2000). Postman suggested that a "medium is a technology within which a culture grows; that is to say, it gives form to a culture's politics, social organization, and habitual ways of thinking" (10). Postman immediately draws forth the importance of media upon culture and organizations. To consider an *ecology*, he returns to Aristotle, who understood it as "household." For Postman, ecology can refer to an environment. Specifically, however, by intertwining media with ecology, Postman suggests that "we are not simply interested in media, but in the ways in which the interaction between media and human beings gives a culture its character and, one might say, help a culture to maintain symbolic balance" (11). Media shapes and frames the cultural, social, and communicative environment.

While media ecologists concern themselves with studying the broad communicative impacts of media on the environment, this also melts into branding and marketing messaging in the public sphere. Corporate communication and IMC are both strategic *communicative* practices that consider the persuasive elements needed to reach audiences; these are inevitably impacted by a technologically infused communicative landscape. The practices of marketing communication in this historical moment have witnessed a rise in an emphasis on branding as a cultivating factor in relationship maintenance between organization and stakeholder, and this is further emphasized with the ease of communication through technologies.

In a technological age, defined by the ways in which communication technologies shape our relationships with others, brands and companies must meet the moment by engaging this environment. IMC, as a whole, is situated as the external communication from brands to their audiences and back. Two-way communication in this model is uniquely essential, and impacted by media ecology in holistic ways. However, corporate communication, a strategic communication management orientation with impacts on both internal and external audiences, must also be sensitive to the impacts of media on the public sphere. Given this brief introduction to the scholarly coordinates to studying the impacts of media on communication, we take seriously the assumption that media shapes the environment, including the environment of the public sphere that is impacted by corporate communication and IMC strategies. The next section, dedicated to an overview of corporate communication in a technological age, suggests that companies and brands must respond to a technological environment that fundamentally changes the structure of internal communication. Such changes necessitate attending to audiences beyond stakeholders in impactful and important ways.

CORPORATE COMMUNICATION IN A
TECHNOLOGICAL AGE: ENGAGING AUDIENCE

This section provides an overview of corporate communication in a technological age. Specific attention is given to the role that corporate social responsibility (CSR) plays within corporate communication. Even though CSR is connected to corporate communication, IMC professionals *must* include CSR in branding practices. This necessity is demonstrative of how communications technologies have shifted the practices; the expectations of audiences are different because the environment is different. Audiences expect more from brands; therefore, brands are being held much more accountable today. More specifically, with global attention being directed toward the weight CSR has on purchasing decisions, companies and brands must reconsider the CSR initiatives and strategies with audiences specifically creating demands and expectations surrounding this issue.

In "A Literature Review of the History and Evolution of Corporate Social Responsibility," Latapí Agudelo, Jóhannsdóttir, and Davidsdóttir (2019) trace the evolution of CSR and identify the most relevant factors that have shaped the understanding of and definition of what it means for a company to be socially responsible. The authors position CSR's first structured definitional rise during the 1930s due to social responsibility debates in the private sector (15). Previously, in the 1920s, companies started considering responsibility, and, more specifically, how to strike a balance between maximizing profits and developing and maintaining client relations (5; Carroll 2008). Companies then moved to adopt social and economic responsibilities (5; Carroll 2008; Heald 1970).

Latapí Agudelo, Jóhannsdóttir, and Davidsdóttir (2019) point to Bowen (1953) as an exemplar of the shifting orientations toward CSR in corporate life. Specifically, Bowen (1953) defined social responsibilities as "the obligations of businessmen to pursue those policies, to make those decisions, or to follow those lines of action which are desirable in terms of the objectives and values of our society" (qtd. in Latapí Agudelo, Jóhannsdóttir, and Davidsdóttir 2019, 6). The emphasis is on companies to improve the business response to social impact. Following this, in the 1960s, a natural understanding of the awareness in society along with social movements called forth a necessity for organizations to be more socially responsible (6). By the end of the 1960s, the social and cultural norms that existed alongside organizations and companies placed significant "pressure" on those organizations to attend to current "expectations" (6; Waterhouse 2017). The emphasis on these social expectations gave way to the 1970s focus on social movements and environmental regulations.

During the 1970s, companies felt more pressure to take on increased responsibilities to society, looking toward human behavior and cultural norms as a marker for corporate behavior (Latapí Agudelo, Jóhannsdóttir, and Davidsdóttir 2019, 6). Carroll (2015) called this period "managing corporate social responsibility" and, in 1979, proposed a new definition of CSR (88). Carroll states: "The social responsibility of business encompasses the economic, legal, ethical, and discretionary expectations that society has of organizations at a given point in the time" (2015, 500). CSR's focus on social movements and environmental regulations in the 1970s influenced CSR practices moving forward (500).

The 1980s undertook ways to implement CSR, and the 1990s saw continued growth in the formalizing of CSR in corporate life (Latapí Agudelo, Jóhannsdóttir, and Davidsdóttir 2019, 8). During this time there was a shift to focusing on different interest groups, and the term "stakeholder" became "common" vernacular (7; Carroll 2008; Wankel 2008). Particularly relevant, with an increased formalization, CSR began to factor into internal and external communication as well as organizational culture and decision-making, directly pointing to a new consideration of societal concerns and expectations of corporate behavior of the time (7). Scholars and companies in the 1990s began to focus on social responsibility and sustainable development. This allowed for new and additional discussions related to audiences, performance, and corporate citizenship leading to uncertainty around the definition of CSR by the end of the decade (7).

In the 2000s two major coordinates emerged around CSR, which included the strategic approach to CSR and the creations of shared values (Latapí Agudelo, Jóhannsdóttir, and Davidsdóttir 2019, 9). The strategic approach to CSR meant a company now needed to make social issues part of its strategies—corporate and communicative (11; Lantos 2001; Carroll 1998). In this way, "CSR responds to the implicit social contract between business and society and can become strategic when it is part of the company's management plan for generating profits" (11; Lantos 2001). This type of strategic response opens up implementing strategic CSR as part of brand management (Latapí Agudelo et al. 2019, 11). Brand management is a strategic necessity, particularly in IMC, and maintaining CSR initiatives and efforts assists in branding efforts.

The creation of shared values is the second major coordinate that emerges in the 2000s around CSR. The concept of shared values and CSR is most notably defined by Porter and Kramer (2011) as "policies and operating practices that enhance the competitiveness of a company while simultaneously advancing economic and social conditions in the communities in which it operates. Shared value creation focuses on identifying and expanding the connections between societal and economic progress" (qtd. in Latapí Agudelo, Jóhannsdóttir, and Davidsdóttir 2019). Here the focus is for companies to use CSR to create shared value. The idea of shared value is grounded in companies now communicating social and global issue concerns in their corporate activities regardless of whether the activities align with the core business practices (2019, 13; Trapp 2012). Still today, the main objective of CSR appears to be around social responsibilities; however, what those responsibilities are is still debated. By providing this historical account of CSR we offer ways to understand corporate communication in a technological age.

Technology is creating a new landscape for corporate communication practices. Today, companies are increasingly needing to consider new technological advances as part of general business activities, and, more specifically, practices grounded in CSR frameworks and strategies (Latapí Agudelo, Jóhannsdóttir, and Davidsdóttir 2019, 20). As a company considers technological advances, it must also maintain a "holistic framework" based on "social responsibility" (20). Organizational branding has changed and is now more so than ever taking on a human characteristic in technology, specifically focusing on how communication technologies have shifted the practices as consumer expectations are different. For example, consider the virtual assistant. Voice technologies, specifically "smart speakers," such as Amazon Echo, Apple Home Pod, and Google Home, offer a wide array of entertainment, but also help users around the house and to purchase goods and services. With a simple, "Hey Google, set the timer for ten minutes," and a reply from Google, "OK," a person knows dinner will not burn. Or, "Hey Alexa, order items in my shopping cart," and a person's Amazon items are on the way. The ability to have a conversation with the AI technology humanizes the brand—the technology is no longer the brand name (i.e., Amazon Echo), but Alexa. Technology companies continue to work to keep up with this innovation, improving the human characteristic in the technology. Moreover, companies and brands across categories are embracing the ideals of technological innovation to meet consumer demand and expectations. In doing so, companies are also faced with finding balance between excess and deficiency related to the level of human interaction and the ethical implications that come with these smart technologies.

In postmodernity, there are multiple ethical positions that frame human communication patterns. This has influenced the ways in which audiences beyond traditional stakeholders look at companies. Moreover, the way companies are connected to legitimacy has changed with social and economic theory. Socio-economic theory announces there are more things to look at other than the shareholders and helps move the discussion to engaging audiences. For example, Ben & Jerry's core values and care and concern for the environment demonstrate moving beyond shareholders to engage audiences. Ben & Jerry's communicates on its website: "Guided by our Core Values, we seek in all we do, at every level of our business, to advance human rights and dignity, support social and economic justice for historically marginalized communities, and protect and restore the Earth's natural system. In other words, we use ice cream to change the world" ("We Believe" n.d.). The Ben & Jerry's website also includes a list of issues it cares about, and how the company is taking action. As an example, Ben & Jerry's states it cares about "climate justice" and has put in place a "climate strategy" that in the short term has helped reduce greenhouse emissions with its ice cream production and includes long-term efforts such as "100% renewable energy by 2025" ("We Believe" n.d.). Ben & Jerry's also includes additional resources for people interested in learning more about how they can help support an issue. An audience, as previously discussed, is any group or individual who can be affected by organizational purpose and objectives, with the potential to affect the actions of a company. As illustrated by the Ben & Jerry's example, through its corporate communication, companies can communicate consistent corporate social responsibility initiatives and, at the same time, move discussions and engage audiences beyond traditional stakeholders.

Generally speaking, audiences, like stakeholders, can be the means in which a company can achieve its ends (e.g., financially and holistically). However, it is normative to say a company does not adopt trends situated within various audiences purely to reach an end. When a company manages its audiences, it must adopt the strategic communicative framework of recognizing that it exists beyond just creating wealth. CSR initiatives illuminate the responsibility of companies to accept accountability for actions that have deeply social and cultural implications. Though sometimes cited as a trend, companies assume responsibility in managing their relationships with their audiences. Particularly in a digital age, audiences—including current and potential consumers—are framing CSR as a priority *for* companies, and expecting those CSR initiatives to be present in all branding activities (an essential component to keep in mind for IMC professionals).

It is important for companies to interrogate their responsiveness to the historical moment, which also requires thoughtfulness in discernment of current trends in the marketplace. However, industry professionals necessarily must separate responsiveness to the historical moment and to trends by virtue of human communication. Being responsible to a historical moment acts as a communicative question: What cultural, social, and ethical value is being emphasized at this time? Being responsive to a trend is exists as *pure* communicative response: What does this organization have to say as a result of this conversation in the public sphere? It is therefore essential to not confuse trend with historical moment. There are many communicative ways to respond to the historical moment, but a company must determine the most appropriate way to position its brand in the marketplace. Simões and Sebastiani (2017) note that companies "that present a strong corporate-sustainability profile attain higher business, social, and environmental performance" (424). The emphasis upon CSR within both corporate communication practices and IMC efforts demonstrates a "both/and" approach to the historical moment and trend distinction. Through the example of adopting CSR strategies, a company can fundamentally manage its identity, mission, and reputation with audiences. In a technological age, human beings are able to have a hand in that formation.

Simões and Sebastiani (2017) connect identity and "corporate sustainability" (424). In defining corporate sustainability, the authors emphasize the integration of cultural, social, environmental, and human concerns into business practices (424). The authors also note that identity is "integrated corporate posture" that has "strategic" and "instrumental" structures that help a company to "define" itself (424). Thus, identity is based on limits, and a company works within those limits. For example, if a company focuses on identity over time, even with cultural changes, the company *should* still maintain its original identity. When a company is in the midst of change, however, it must determine what its focus will be on with identity.

For example, in February 2014, CVS Caremark made the decision to cease selling tobacco products. CNN reported that Larry J. Merlo, president and CEO of CVS Caremark in 2014, stated that "ending the sale of cigarettes and tobacco products at CVS/pharmacy is the right thing for us to do for our customers and our company to help people on their path to better health. . . . Put simply, the sale of tobacco products is inconsistent with our purpose" (Landau 2014). Later that year, CVS Caremark rebranded to CVS Health. This was intended to "reflect its broader health care commitment and its expertise in driving the innovations needed to shape the future of health" (CVS Health 2014). This move fundamentally shifted CVS Health's identity, its impact on audiences, and its branding tactics. However, the move also reflected a *focus* in its mission that responded to CSR initiatives related to public health. CVS Health repositioned its brand in a different light for audiences, met the historical moment, and yet retained elements of its identity along the way.

Corporate communication in a technological age responds to relationships with consumers through responsiveness *and* communication. Because of the influx of communication technologies, as we argue, today, companies have "control of communication while various constituencies, competitors, and the general public have greater access to information and to employees at all levels within companies" (Argenti 2006, 358). The assumption of two-way communication that is emphasized in IMC, and that will be discussed further in this chapter, is a direct result of a changing communicative landscape. Furthermore, a technological communicative landscape promotes instantaneous dialogue between audiences and companies, eliminating one-way communication typically associated with marketing and communication behaviors. Audiences, more so than ever, expect information to be provided accurately and immediately.

For example, in March 2012, *Oracle* published a survey that reported that "81% of Twitter users expect a same-day response to questions and complaints posted at the newsfeed" (6). In 2022, the Sprout Social Index reported that that percentage had evolved to 13% expecting a response *within the first hour* (Sprout Social n.d.). Moreover, in asking survey respondents how they felt about the statement, "It is important for brands to raise awareness and take a stand on sensitive topics," 34% strongly agreed, 37% agreed, and 22% remained neutral; only 7% did not expect to hear the "voices" of their favorite brands on social issues (Sprout Social n.d.). Immediacy, transparency, and communication are expectations that brands cannot step away from.

The practices of corporate communication in a technological age continue to experience an increase in the need for immediacy as it pertains to responding to audiences. However, as Argenti (2006) suggests, "although the Internet allows companies to present their viewpoints directly to key constituents, control over information dissemination is lost" (359). For example, a person can send out a "tweet" on Twitter and, in seconds, other people can respond before the company can reply to/address the communication. The number of communication channels also contributes to the lack of control (359). Moreover, the task of a company is to navigate and be a viable company. To do so, companies will move forward with transparency. Transparency can offer significant benefits, but *must* be exercised with an element of restraint. With transparency, a company risks losing the understanding of what is needed and not needed. Companies *must* be clear in corporate communication practice about what kind of information needs to be communicated to audiences. The increasing demands of transparency via digital communication technologies from human beings puts organizations in a delicate position; maintaining transparency, for example, about CSR initiatives, must be balanced with sensitive information that should not always be shared publicly.

Technology advancements bring both new opportunities and challenges for companies and their corporate communication. For example, on November 30, 2022, ChatGPT, a chatbot, was launched by OpenAI, an artificial intelligence research company. The chatbot is a generative AI tool designed to interact with human beings in a conversational way. The user enters a written prompt and ChatGPT responds with a "human-like text or images and videos" (Browne 2023). ChatGPT is different from other generative AI tools because it "is powered by a large language model, or LLM, meaning it's programmed to understand human language and generate responses based on large corpora of data" (Browne 2023). No previous generative AI tool has become so influential and used by consumers and businesses in such a short time. Within the first week of its launch, ChatGPT had one million users and 100 million monthly active users within two months ("About" OpenAI 2023). As a CNBC article noted, "It took TikTok nine months to reach 100 million users and Instagram two and a half years" (Browne 2023). The tool's popularity has caused a firestorm of both positive and negative conversations in industry, leading some companies to embrace employees' use of ChatGPT and others to ban it completely from the workplace. Companies in support of using the tool in the workplace see it as a way to increase employee productivity. A concern of companies that do not favor using ChatGPT in the workplace is the risk of making public sensitive company information.

ChatGPT is just one example of technological advancements impacting a company's corporate communication. In considering the profound implications of introducing AI technologies in internal communication, the ideals and values of organizational culture are called into question when, for example, sensitive information is placed into a virtual platform. Moreover, strong human communication concerns surrounding culture may evolve in recognizing that AI may or may not replace face-to-face communication that can, and should, foster healthy cultures and climates. Today's companies are faced with radical innovations that push technology to new levels, and, as a result, changes the way companies engage audiences beyond traditional stakeholders.

In *The Human Condition*, Hannah Arendt (1958) calls attention to the first human protection that technology puts at risk, the separation of public and private. Technology has allowed companies to use corporate communication to engage audiences beyond traditional stakeholders, but has also created new challenges for companies with the advent of the internet, and, more specifically, social media. The need to integrate all corporate communication activities to reach audiences beyond traditional stakeholders puts at risk the separation of public and private today more than in the past. More so, the need for enhanced corporate communication related to CSR has become more crucial to ensure a company's survival. Examining corporate communication within the digital framework while attempting to focus on the customer, company, brand, technology, and strategy, offers an explanation as to what is needed to implement a corporate communication strategy today. Knowing *what* the corporate communication process is and *how* to construct it, however, does not explain *why* companies should do it. Moreover, and as noted in the above section, corporate communication practices have not only been influenced *by* technology but also by the emphasis on IMC in a technological age. Though corporate communication remains a separate and distinct communication function, IMC and branding have infiltrated most communication efforts. As noted through the CSR example, branding efforts must also be cognizant of corporate communication efforts as consumers are making purchasing decisions based upon these elements. We now turn to IMC to further emphasize how technologies have invited this important communicative change.

IMC IN A TECHNOLOGICAL AGE: TECHNOLOGY AND BRANDING

As noted in the example of CSR initiatives, communication between brands and audiences has significantly increased in previous years. Even more than the increase in communication is the changing expectations that audiences demonstrate in connection with brand efforts. The rise of IMC, as discussed in previous chapters, pinpoints an essential turn in marketplace practices as it relates to human communication. Now more so than ever, human beings are empowered to create brand experiences in connection with the brand itself. No longer can organizations create media messages that then impact consumers and audiences extending beyond traditional stakeholders. Consumers also participate in the brand experience, and therefore offer voices and perspectives that shape the brand itself. This is, primarily, a result of changing communication technologies that permit an ease and immediacy related to consumer voices in the production and dissemination of marketing messages. While elucidated throughout the corporate communication section on CSR, IMC takes up the call to respond to consumer demands that shape both business strategies and communication initiatives.

Luxton, Reid, and Mavondo (2015) note that the marketplace environment is specifically multifaceted, complex, and *changing*, creating opportunities and, perhaps, threats that industry professionals must respond to. More specifically, because of this evolving landscape, brands "offer value in terms of the perceived credibility and trustworthiness of the firm" in order "for emotional attachment to form between" organizations and audiences, thus leading to long-term brand loyalty and a push for consumers to *act* in a way that is mutually beneficial to brand and stakeholder alike (38). IMC scholarship and practices respond to the emotional connection of branding with consumers, perhaps even more prevalent in our historical moment that so easily embraces two-way communication via the efficiency of communication technologies.

In the early 1990s, as IMC was first new and pushing toward integration in the midst of an evolving landscape, Kit Yarrow (2014) noted that the word "web" meant little more than something "with a spider," and, in 1995, the word "Amazon" may simply have referred to a "river" (12). Yarrow suggests that the new consumer mindset demands attentiveness from advertisers and marketers (IMC professionals). Yarrow (1958–2020), a nationally renowned consumer psychologist and professor, was widely regarded for her research into consumer behavior. In 2015, the American Psychological Association noted that Yarrow believed that brands and "retailers" who would continue to thrive in a changing digital landscape are those that "appreciate their shoppers' potent desire for engaging and validating experience in the marketplace" (O'Hara 2017). While much can be pointed to in terms of scholarship on the intersection of IMC and technology, Yarrow's work specifically addresses the move toward engaging audiences beyond stakeholders.

As Yarrow (2014) suggests, "In a marketplace flooded with solutions, the particular products and brands that consumers choose will be selected because they satisfy and address a new consumer psychology," particularly a new consumer psychology driven by a push for innovation amid a distracted and emotional communicative environment plagued by isolation (5). For Yarrow, consumers are emotional consumers; within this new technology environment, practitioners must contend with new expectations to engage with audiences across communication platforms. However, today's consumer is characterized by an influx of psychological emotions and communicative behaviors that are connected to the rise of communication technologies in this historical moment. Yarrow among others (i.e., Schultz & Schultz 2004; Turkle 2015; Rushkoff 2013) draw insight from and investigate the significant role of technologies in shaping consumptive patterns and behaviors. IMC offers a bridge between these human communication patterns to address new paths forward.

Yarrow (2014) notes that consumers are increasingly preoccupied with the new and the innovative. In fact, consumers today focus on the innovative and the new, which is subsequently "bolstered through the consumer championship and trust building of social media, rating, and review sites. Products can go from introduction to popularity at an unprecedented rate through the reach and reassurance provided by social media" (15–16). Because of this, IMC requires an unprecedented attentiveness to two-way communication and dialogue that emphasizes the relationship building present in IMC, expanding audiences beyond traditional stakeholders *and* responding to an ever-changing landscape. To be innovative means to respond to both the market and consumer demand—a process that is holistically addressed by IMC strategies and tactics.

This demand for innovation does not solely focus on the *already* techno-logically advanced products, services, and brands that characterize our cur-rent marketplace. Yarrow (2014) cites Adidas's "wall of virtual footwear" as an example of the demand for innovation that extends beyond the product itself (17). The desire to identify innovation has begun holistically to shape advertising, marketing, and public relations tactics. This translates into a communication perspective by which consumers have created structural expectations over values that brands should be speaking about and interacting with their consumers over. Yarrow suggests that consumers are increasingly engaging in communication not just with brands but with other consumers to generate brand loyalty outside of the traditional brand-consumer relationship. Yarrow writes that consumers have now been empowered to communicate their expectations for their brands (21). Because the consumer is so very influential in this historical moment, relationships have evolved with cultural and social expectations of immediacy and efficiency and are specifically tied to the communication of value in the marketplace.

In our current historical moment, the ability to be siloed acts in direct opposition to the integration needed to develop relationships with audiences and to maintain those relationships in real and meaningful ways. Bruhn and Schnebelen (2015) note that the "emergence of the internet provided the stimulus for substantial changes in the communication landscape" (465). More specifically, this introduction of two-way communication offers a shift in the consumer-brand relationship whereby there exists mutually beneficial communicative values in the branding process. For example, Bruhn and Schnebelen note that, for brands, communication technologies and social media in particular can assist in "fostering relationships, interacting with all stakeholders, . . . influencing customer perceptions and gaining customer insights" (465). Moreover, for consumers, social media and communication technologies empower consumers to "create their own contents, to express their opinions and to obtain free and easy access to a wide range of product and brand information that facilitate their purchase decisions" (465). Booking sites, such as Airbnb and Booking.com, illustrate empowering consumers. For example, Airbnb allows reviews for stays. Hosts and guests can leave reviews for stays that have been booked and paid for on Airbnb. In doing so, Airbnb works to ensure a "fair review system" that "protects our com-munity's genuine feedback" ("Help Center" 2023). Both hosts and guests have fourteen days to submit a review once checkout is complete, and the reviews are not posted until both parties submit a review or the review period ends ("Help Center" 2023). While reviews are not moderated, Airbnb has review policies, and if the host or guest violates a policy the review may be removed ("Help Center" 2023). Arguably, allowing both hosts and guests to leave reviews increases customer perceptions and provides invaluable customer insights. Customer reviews are just one of many examples of why and how empowering communicative techniques are an important factor in understanding IMC today.

In his work *Present Shock: When Everything Happens Now*, Douglas Rushkoff (2013) further expands upon the impact of technology upon the consumer mentality. He notes that "the consumer lives in a present made possible by the temporal compression of others. He can consume something in minutes that may have taken months to manufacture and transport" (165). Moreover, Rushkoff comments that advertisers as a whole "feed us the mythology of a brand so that it is spring-loaded into our psyche—read to emerge fully formed when we see the label in the store" (167). He says that the goal of consumption in today's historical moment is to never make the consumer holistically satisfied—because we need people to keep consuming. But time compression acts as a way to ensure that this happens. There is no time between consumption and emotional resolution; thus, the act of purchasing is more "rewarding"—and all to do with a preemptive formation of the brand prior to even encountering the purchase point (167). For Rushkoff, the phrase "act now" "simply means there's an opportunity to do something at a particular moment. To be a part of something. Or simply, to *do* something. Just as midcentury mass-produced goods now feel historical and authentic to us, there's a sense that reaching the crest of current innovation or style will keep us authentic to the now" (168). Rushkoff's important points find resonance within Yarrow's work, as well.

For Yarrow (2014), the current technological landscape has inundated human beings with overstimulation. These important social and communication trends have been directly addressed by many scholars and media ecologists alike (Postman, Rushkoff, Turkle, etc.). However, Yarrow brings this back to IMC and suggests that one cannot remove the communicative changes in the cultural environment from the practices within IMC itself. For Yarrow, "our brains typically delegate the processing of nonverbal messages to the unconscious mind; this is why symbolic communication has always been an especially potent marketing communication tool" (35). She notes that this unconscious process, traditionally, directly influences and resonates with the emotional side of our being. Thus, in Aristotle's *ethos, pathos,* and *logos* (1999), the emphasis on *pathos* is a natural move in that it is where human beings can unconsciously process images and symbols at exceptional speeds and *still* find influence in them (Yarrow 2014, 35).

IMC as a marketplace practice is focused on relationship building and branding that finds *connection with* consumers through various platforms. Yet

Yarrow (2014) notes that the technological environment has fundamentally shifted the ways in which human beings strive to make connections. Yarrow comments that "for many the cellphone has become an adult binky" (42). Smartphones and devices routinely pull us away from in-person interaction and into the screen. Her analysis suggests that even though we are digitally connected, we have become isolated and increasingly more disconnected in social situations. She notes that "right up there with food, water, and shelter is our need for human connection. It's the foundation of happiness and the source of meaning and purpose in life—yet we've never been more alone" (45). In an individualistic society, our consumption patterns have begun to mimic our emotional and communicative expectations.

For IMC professionals, this social and societal move to radical individualism and isolation results in an individualistic consumer who "wants more attention, personalization, involvement, and appreciation. All of this is made possible by one of the very dividers of society—technology" (Yarrow 2014, 75). Thus, with the new focus on generating brand loyalty and relationship building as a primary factor in successful marketing and advertising efforts, the need to emphasize and personalize communication takes on a new and important role for all institutions in the marketplace. This is because "the partnerships and loyalties consumers once had with brands and retailers are more fragile. The retailers and marketers that succeed truly understand and empathize with their consumers" (77). The way to establish these quite emotional connections is through an attentiveness to communication in a technological environment.

For example, Wendy's use of social media has generated both attention and admiration for its development of its brand personality while simultaneously connecting with audiences that extend beyond its traditional stakeholders. In 2018, *Forbes Magazine* published an article titled "How Wendy's Learned to Stop Worrying and Love Its Twitter Roasts of McDonald's." The author notes that Wendy's is both a "social media darling and a close study of marketers" due to the brand personality that the fast-food chain restaurant has developed as a direct result of its sarcastic Twitter feed (Cheng 2018). Its social media usage has been so popular that the chain has even been receiving inquiries from other brands about how to successfully build such strong rapport with their audiences. Most importantly, however, the article notes that Wendy's social media team "studied the company's advertising history closely to have a uniform voice for the brand identity," a hallmark of strong IMC practices (Cheng 2018). In recognizing the emotional connection with the consumer, Wendy's has managed to retain a number three position in its industry (Cheng 2018).

Yarrow (2014) recognized that the deep-seated cultural changes leading to the rise of the *necessity* of social media come with serious consequences, yet not all is lost. She notes that companies who embrace technological innovation can "up their impact through things like branded apps, advanced displays, superior website experiences, and tie-ins with more technologically oriented brands" (125). Our products and services do not have to change, *but* our communication with consumers ultimately must. Importantly, Yarrow suggests that the dichotomy between online and face-to-face personas is a false distinction—they are integrated. This integrated experience for consumers *also* means that it should be integrated for brands. With the rise of technology comes a push for big data for marketers and advertisers. Yarrow ends her work with hope, suggesting that "big data is not a replacement for creativity or the insights that come from experience. It's great at exploring how consumers are using what you have right now and testing ideas that have been already generated. But it doesn't create the new ideas. So far, that's still a job for humans" (130). In this viewpoint, the embracing of the unavoidable change in the technological communicative environment means that intention and balance are key. Technology does not replace the human—but, when done well and with attentiveness, it can enhance communication *and* meet consumers where they are.

Keeping this key lesson in mind, brands also have a unique opportunity to generate brand trust *through* integration and consistency that are further advanced in this environment. For example, Yarrow (2014) cites the "potential of social media" that allows for "humanizing" brands—a way to generate brand loyalty and trust, making brands more "relatable and genuine" through "anchoring" campaigns and "brand stories" (139). Specifically, consumers in this current marketplace view "the directness and intimacy of social media as access to a brand's soul. That access provides the insight they need to understand the personality and values of a brand—its human characteristics" (141). This is directly possible *because* of the new technological landscape. Allowing for consumer voices to shape and engage with brands and branding practices provides connection that superficially mirrors human relationships in ways that consumers rely upon to make purchasing decisions. Moreover, the move to engaging with audiences beyond stakeholders provides platforms for strong engagement with *human beings* in an age when digital communication technologies and branding remain essential and at the forefront of public sphere practices.

IMPLICATIONS FOR AUDIENCES BEYOND STAKEHOLDERS IN A TECHNOLOGICAL AGE

In a technological age, corporate communication and IMC practices have shifted to account for the voices of audiences with an unprecedented amount of attention and care. Schultz and Schultz (2004) note the shift away from the Four P's of traditional marketing communication—product, price, place, and promotion. This shift is largely due to the lack of emphasis on customers under this model (4). Particularly at the onset of IMC, "product proliferation, a plethora of new channels, and more competitive pricing all demanded new forms and types of marketing communication" (6). Specifically, three cultural shifts in the marketplace during the mid-1980s refocused traditional advertising into IMC-focused practices. Those included "digital technology across the entire spectrum of business operations," an emphasis on *branding* as a "competitive differentiating tool," and globalization, reshaping the structure of the marketplace itself (9). This influx of social and cultural shifts in the marketplace took marketing communication and reshaped its attentiveness and focus to an organizational necessity to continue to foster stakeholder relationships, a key component to corporate communication practices.

More specifically, in this technological age, the emphasis that IMC places on relationship building and dialogue opens up a deepened expectation that audiences beyond traditional stakeholders have on their influence over business practices. For example, in January 2023, Tarte Cosmetics hosted a brand influencer trip to Dubai. Sending popular makeup influencers and their significant others via business class, Tarte Cosmetics spent significant money to host this trip at the Ritz-Carlton Ras Al Khaimah, providing personal villas to the influencers and ensuring that they were met with numerous products and gifts that they would, hopefully, market to their followers (Mendez II 2023). During that weekend, however, audiences beyond Tarte's immediate stakeholders began to post videos on TikTok, lamenting the extravagance of the trip, which audiences immediately labeled as "'tone-deaf' as the United States is on the verge of a recession" (Mendez II 2023). The public outcry was so great that founder and CEO Maureen Kelly made a statement with *Glossy*, noting that Tarte has "long 'prioritized their marketing budget into building relationships with influencers'" (Mendez II 2023). Kelly was also quoted as noting that "'every day, brands make decisions about how to spend their marketing budgets. For some companies, that means a huge Super Bowl commercial or a multi-million dollar contract with a famous athlete or musician'" (Maguire 2023). Regardless, Tarte Cosmetics was essentially forced into discussing corporate communication and IMC practices with audiences outside of its traditional stakeholders to account for a marketing decision. In a technological age, audience voice requires attentiveness and thoughtfulness in communication, as it carries with it the power to shape brand perception.

Corporate communication, which fundamentally deals with the maintenance of stakeholder relationships, has shifted in practices to include an acknowledgment of the formative power of social media upon strategic initiatives to include audiences beyond traditional stakeholders. Additionally,

IMC and branding efforts can also find resonance with audiences beyond traditional stakeholders in a move toward utilizing social media as a relationship-building tool. Moreover, the organizational communication strategies companies and brands implement must acknowledge cultural and social expectations of communication to continue to find positioning in the public sphere. These implications offer theoretical touchpoints for companies and brands to consider when adopting new communication strategies and initiatives to meet the historical moment, reaching audiences beyond traditional stakeholders in a technological age.

Chapter 5

Duolingo and the Voice of the Company

A Case Study in Audiences beyond Stakeholders

In this work, the practices of corporate communication and IMC have been considered to respond directly to a communicative necessity in the marketplace—engaging audiences beyond traditional stakeholders. In both areas of communicative strategies, history, ethics, culture, and the technological environment have been analyzed and discussed to emphasize the distinctive shaping structure of the external environment on the interactions between companies and the various audiences that impact those organizations and institutions. This chapter specifically considers a current case study to further elucidate the profound implications, benefits, and advantages for understanding the move to audiences beyond traditional stakeholders in today's historical moment.

With the rise of communication technologies, particularly those in the realm of social media, companies and brands have been forced to reconsider the audiences that they serve in unique and meaningful ways. For example, author Candice Georgiadis, in May 2022, published an article titled "How Brands Are Capitalizing TikTok to Win New Audiences" with *Entrepreneur* magazine. TikTok broke $1 billion in profits in 2021 and promotes a "relatability" factor that audiences flock to in droves (Georgiadis 2022). For Georgiadis, the ethos of TikTok is a lack of pressure to appear "perfect." Because of that, brands can feel comfortable "showcase[ing] your brand's carefree and fun side" (Georgiadis 2022). Moreover, based on the algorithm present in TikTok's "For You," "your brand can appear on TikTok users' FYP even if they don't follow you" (Georgiadis 2022). This means that even if a user is not actively seeking a company's content or promoting its brand, the company or brand still has the power to impact and to persuade users, a unique communication opportunity for companies and brands in this historical moment.

This chapter offers coordinates for understanding communication strategies in a technological age through focusing upon a primary case study: Duolingo. This work offers Duolingo as an example through which a company and/or brand can recognize the necessity of the integration of history, ethics, culture, and technology in marketplace practices today. Companies and brands can thrive in this new environment by understanding how *human communication*, as a product of these coordinates, changes and, with it, expectations form new guidelines. The chapter posits Duolingo as an exemplar of understanding audiences beyond stakeholders. In reviewing Duolingo's meteoric rise of TikTok fame in the span of just a few short years, this chapter offers implications for understanding how all companies and brands, no matter how large or small, can meet the communicative moment of engaging with audiences beyond traditional stakeholders.

A CASE STUDY IN AUDIENCES BEYOND STAKEHOLDERS: DUOLINGO AND SOCIAL MEDIA

This work has reviewed four major coordinates in the shift to understanding audiences beyond traditional stakeholders in corporate communication and IMC practices: historical development, ethics in engaging audiences, organizational culture, and the rise of communication technologies. Importantly, these coordinates have set the stage for the current communicative environment that companies and brands find themselves working within. This is important to note, as at the beginning of the social media age, so to speak, many companies and brands felt a renewed sense of hope that the call to cultivate relationships with consumers and engage in two-way communication would become easier. After all, social media platforms allowed for a unique back-and-forth that seemed to facilitate those consumer-led expectations.

According to *Harvard Business Review*, in an article by Douglas Holt that appeared in March 2016 titled "Branding in the Age of Social Media: A Better Alternative to Branded Content," when social media first arrived in current culture, companies and brands believed that social media provided them a media-driven means to engage in relationship building specifically between those companies and brands with their consumers without any third-party interference (Holt 2016). However, according to Holt, social media has made brands appear "less significant" in the face of "crowdculture." For Holt, crowdculture refers to a new phenomenon ushered in with digital communication technologies whereby "digital crowds" act as the "public innovators of culture," a unique challenge for brands who "succeed when they break through the culture." Holt explains that branded content is not a new phenomenon. In what he calls the "mass media age," branded content was often modeled after "popular entertainment," an avenue through which companies and brands could fold popular culture into the relationship-building enterprise in a way that resonated with their audiences.

Holt (2016) notes that branded content was simpler in the mass media age because media was, essentially, controlled by a handful of companies. So, when companies wanted to release branding efforts and messaging, the companies had the ability to "buy their way to fame by paying to place their brands in this tightly controlled cultural arena" (Holt 2016). Of course, as time progressed onward, new communication technologies allowed for various audiences to have more control over their entertainment. For example, the Internet and devices like DVR made it easier for consumers to "opt out of ads." So companies and brands were pushed to be even more creative in their persuasion techniques than ever before, and these persuasive communication practices needed to meet the structure of the technologies that their various audiences used to engage both publicly and privately.

Today, social media has fundamentally altered not *just* the structure of culture but the way that culture is generated. Holt (2016) refers to "crowd-culture" to refer to the various subcultures that emerge across Internet and social media platforms related to cultural topics. Furthermore, Holt suggests that these subcultures are creative forces that can shape cultural expectations in significant ways. Persuasion is emerging from audiences themselves. For example, Holt comments that in "YouTube or Instagram rankings of channels by numbers of subscribers, corporate brands barely appear. Only three have cracked the YouTube Top 500" (Holt 2016). Social media has privileged the *person*, rather than a company. And Holt notes that, because of this, companies and brands need to be aware that consumers are wary of persuasion from brands over these platforms, considering content, often, as "brand spam." In a technological age, where relationships can be cultivated between companies and brands and its audiences, consumers are not interested in traditional persuasion from companies.

Holt (2016) comments that "celebrities are all garnering the superengaged community that pundits have long promised social media would deliver. But it's not available to companies and their branded goods and services." However, Holt offers an alternative that he terms "cultural branding," which essentially means that a brand "promotes an innovative ideology that breaks with category conventions." In this approach, brands actively promote values and ideals that audiences are actively searching for that they cannot find in the current marketplace. Holt's example is the food industry, where audiences push for cleaner eating and better alternatives to ingredients used in both restaurants and grocery stores alike. He notes that Chipotle from 2011–2013 successfully attended to this push that emerged through conversations related to "farm-to-table" sourcing. By providing things like videos that demonstrated its commitment to this ideology, Chipotle emerged victorious in that it spoke to a cultural trend that was being discussed beyond its traditional stakeholders. An entire subculture addressed this concern, and Chipotle offered branded content that resonated with audiences beyond those stakeholders.

Holt (2016) contends that this can be a "double-edged sword. The brand has to walk the walk or it will be called out." While Holt specifically offers ways to capitalize on his notion of crowdculture, and suggests strategies for how brands can fundamentally enact similar campaigns, Holt's contribution to this work lies in his holistic emphasis on the need to understand the *human* communication happening across these digital platforms. More specifically, companies and brands should attend to their corporate communication from an IMC perspective and move beyond traditional stakeholders. In today's current climate driven by social media platforms, listening to and engaging with audiences beyond stakeholders are impactful and important actions for companies and brands to take. Holt, when concluding his article, reminds us that companies have the power to "tap into the power of the crowd" in this historical moment. The crowd, however, is not simply one primary audience that a company or brand is dealing with—the crowd is a number of audiences and peoples that need to be both acknowledged and considered in developing communication strategies.

On social media sites in particular, ideologies and conversations happen that impact consumer psychology extending beyond a company's traditional set of stakeholders. More specifically, these conversations can influence global perception of companies. For example, in July 2022, influencers Kylie Jenner and Kim Kardashian critiqued Meta-owned Instagram for attempting to model its platform too closely to TikTok. According to *Business Insider*'s Travis Clark (2022), this could be problematic for Meta, considering that these two influencers boast over 600 million followers between the two and, in years past, their critique has led to dropping stocks. This means that the voices of audiences, stakeholders or otherwise, have significant impact when raised over these platforms. Moreover, while the social media landscape is still unfolding, some companies and brands have not only capitalized on the use of these platforms but uniquely positioned themselves in a way to reach audiences beyond traditional stakeholders in engaging and necessary ways through attentiveness to the *communicative value* of generating content for technological environments today.

Today, social media platforms are flooded with paid posts and content, advertising, and marketing campaigns. Because of this, companies and brands feel intense and important pressure to ensure that audiences remain invested in posted content, contributing extensively to both a corporate communication perspective with regard to corporate identity, image, and reputation as well as an IMC perspective associated with brand loyalty and brand equity. Many brands are aware of the need to take on this new approach in order to continue to reach audiences. Duolingo, in particular, has generated a voice on its platforms that specifically responds to this call.

Duolingo, headquartered in Pittsburgh, Pennsylvania, is a technology company that is primarily known for its app designed as a language-education course. The company was founded in 2011 by CEO Luis von Ahn and CTO Severin Hacker, employing approximately 550 individuals (Doughty 2021). The employee number also includes global social media manager Zaria Parvez. The company's interactive app offers courses in a number of different languages, for a number of different levels, and is structured as an educational tool that mirrors a social networking design but that promotes an accessible (and affordable) entrance into learning language. Duolingo markets its mission as centered upon the goal to "develop the best education in the world and make it universally available" (Duolingo 2022). The company has since moved into math-based education courses and works routinely to continue to promote innovative programming that simultaneously delivers upon the values of free and accessible.

In the promotion of a podcast titled "Young Influentials," author Colin Daniels published an article in *AdWeek* on Duolingo's unique approach to utilizing its social media platforms. Daniels noted that "what makes DuoLingo stand out on the platform is how its social strategy doesn't involve constantly promoting itself, but finding ways to connect with those familiar with the service and those who are not" (Daniels 2022). The brand heavily relies upon popular culture and the use of humor to reach its audiences, and to great success. The company received the Ad Age's Creativity Awards' Social Marketer of the Year in 2022 (Wheless 2022). In a March 2022 article in *Teen Vogue*, author Lauren Rearick highlighted the global social media manager for Duolingo, Zaria Parvez, and her innovative approach to representing the brand on social media platforms, particularly TikTok. In the article, Parvez notes that "Duolingo's whole personality has been about making language learning fun and doing fun things. . . . Duolingo's culture has never been very buttoned up." In engaging a "fun" new voice on social media platforms, Parvez suggests that it is still quite "on brand," though, perhaps, not traditional marketing and advertising outside of a digital age—the company is targeting audiences beyond stakeholders.

And it works. According to an article in *Fast Company*, since 2021, Duolingo has gained 4 million followers on TikTok, "routinely fetches more than 1 million views per video," and currently boasts over 500 million downloads of its app with $250 million in revenue during the year 2021

(Honigman 2022). This is essential. For Hernandez-Fernandez and Lewis (2019), "consumers look for brands that are relevant and increasingly search for authenticity in brands" (222). Similarly, in looking at "brand authenticity," the authors note that audiences are interested in claims of authenticity as it relates to both values and "non-commercial differentiation" over product persuasion (224). This is, furthermore, important because audiences are drawn to a move beyond purchasing for the sake of consumption. The authors note that audiences find connections between the things that they buy with the authentic nature of the "places, history, [and] culture" associated with the object itself (225). In their study, Hernandez-Fernandez and Lewis found that "individuality, consistency, and continuity effectively capture and positively influence consumer perceptions of BA [brand authenticity] and that a higher consumer's perception of brand authenticity resulting in higher perceived value and brand trust" (233). When a brand is able to effectively position itself with audiences to be authentic, human, and intentional, consumers place greater value upon the brand itself. This leads to better relationships (a staple in IMC) but, also, to a better profit.

Meeting the bottom line is often consider the primary goal of companies by consumers. However, Duolingo's approach arguably places sentiment (the relationship with consumers) over rationality (making a profit), providing insight into its corporate culture and values. Deal and Kennedy (2000) articulate a view that strong communication and strong values make better companies. More specifically, companies do not have to have the same values, but companies have to have a commitment to values. The biggest quality issue in any company is the people. Employees are the most responsible, and communication is intensely important to how any company can function and maintain its brand, image, and reputation. As Van Riel and Fombrun (2007) state, "'corporate reputation' is a multi-stakeholder construct that is particularly appropriate for measuring the effectiveness of an organization's communication system" (39). Traditionally, corporate reputation was understood as the overall opinion of companies by stakeholders (Van Riel and Fombrun 2007). However, consumers today have moved from being solely consumers of a product to also being interested in building relations with other consumers (Christensen, Torp, and Firat 2005; Cova 1996). As Cornelissen (2000) points out, corporate communication *must* "understand the dynamics of stakeholder involvement and communicative behavior as it relates to the new media landscape" (i.e., social media) (119). Consequently, a greater focus is placed on the audience beyond the traditional stakeholder relationship.

Parvez's approach has generated a singular spotlight on Duolingo's social media presence, and the power of social media to cultivate a relationship with audiences beyond traditional stakeholders. Taking Holt's work into account, Duolingo recognized a cultural ideology of humanizing brands to the extent that the global marketplace often expects companies and brands to *be* culturally aware, even when a company may or may not be culturally relevant. Cornelissen (2000) connects this type of position to a need for companies to consider their "behavioral actions" in their corporate communication (119). Establishing good relationships with audiences goes beyond the buying and selling of a product or service. Parvez and her team continue to promote "unhinged" content that still seems to represent the brand Duolingo in meaningful ways. *Marketing Magazine* noted that Parvez's initial strategy of experimentally creating a "sitcom series" of the unhinged character of Duo, the green owl, is "better advertising" because "it is getting more eyes on their product, and more investment in the content and creators themselves" (Vaughn 2022). Simply put, Parvez's approach highlights the necessity of recognizing the power of reaching beyond traditional stakeholders to continue to spread awareness of your brand while simultaneously creating new opportunities to cultivate relationships with audiences through corporate communication.

Corporate communication traditionally takes an organizational approach showing concern for how to manage a company's image and reputation (Cornelissen 2000). Parvez's strategy, however, is both a public and private obligation to the company and the brand as well as consumers. In an article for the online publication *DigiDay*, McCoy (2021) cites Parvez as noting that part of her job is to spend *hours* scrolling through social media. Why? She believes that part of her role is to engage in "social listening." Moreover, she and her team spend hours responding to posts from commenters and audiences alike. More specifically, however, Parvez has utilized TikTok as a primary vehicle for this work. In this way, her team can respond not only with written posts but with full videos that continue to offer easier access to the brand's identity and voice. In offering advice in the *Teen Vogue* article, Parvez is quoted as noting that "another big skill that social people need to have is empathy. I mean that in the sense of being aware of the difference audiences you're speaking to, being able to walk in someone else's shoes, and understanding that what works for one audience might not work for another" (Rearick 2022). Duolingo's TikTok account has been framed "less about selling Duolingo to TikTok audiences, who notoriously don't want to be sold to," and more about "entertaining them." And according to Brendan Gahan, who is a chief social officer at Mekanism creative agency, "it's the humanization of Duo that seems to be the selling point" (McCoy 2021). Of course, Duolingo is not the only company or brand to successfully humanize itself with this sort of approach (e.g., CarMax, Chewy, or Southwest Airlines). However, its notable attitude toward engaging consumers beyond traditional marketing techniques is an important case study in corporate communication and IMC in a technological age, particularly in demonstrating the importance of corporate values and branding efforts.

This approach certainly comes with risks, specifically that "being silly on social media is risky and can backfire if not done with intention, buy-in from leadership, and self-awareness" (Honigman 2019). In May 2022, the Duolingo app faced immediate backlash after responding on TikTok to a post by NBC related to Amber Heard, who had been in court with her ex-husband, Johnny Depp, in a defamation lawsuit. The brand posted the comment "Ya'll think Amber watches TikTok" on a clip of Ms. Heard testifying under oath about alleged incidents of domestic violence while still married to Mr. Depp. Then twenty-four-year-old Parvez issued an immediate apology, noting that as a young recent college graduate who was shocked by the level of engagement Duolingo's social media had gotten *after* adopting this approach to its social media voice, she was still learning how to appropriately manage that responsibility (Bradley 2022). Many voices continue to express anger in this clear misstep, noting that to make a joke related to the case was extraordinarily problematic given its sensitive nature regarding domestic violence. Others offer words of wisdom in moving forward. Bradley (2022) notes that Steak-umm social media manager Nathan Allebach suggested that "The social media manager made a mistake by jumping in. . . . They deleted the comment and owned it. Pushing boundaries is always a risk. It's easy to get lost in the sauce when you're at the top of the game." Others, including Ravel Wilson, who is a social media strategist for M1 Finance, noted that it is "unrealistic for social media managers to know something is a mistake inherently when they do it" (Bradley 2022). In this conversation, however, the line between brand voice and persuasion is still untenable and uncertain.

In this event, and particularly for crisis communication, Coombs and Holladay (2012) define paracrisis as "a publicly visible crisis threat that charges an organization with irresponsible or unethical behavior" (409). For Duolingo and Parvez, the decision to continue to engage in "unhinged content" that extended to a comment on the Amber Heard and Johnny Depp defamation case resulted in a paracrisis, where corporate communication was strategically needed to protect the brand and to allow for continued IMC efforts that engaged with audiences beyond their traditional stakeholders.

Yet, even in the misstep, many lessons can be learned by the strategic attention placed on communication in a technological age. Parvez noted that TikTok, in particular, was generated "for people to have fun" (Doughty 2021). Because of that, when brands utilize *this* platform, "brands are there to entertain, they're not there just to sell—brands that try selling things don't really tend to resonate'" (Doughty 2021). Michaela Kron, Duolingo's marketing lead in the United States, is quoted in this same article as saying, "It's really just about entertaining, having fun, building up the brand, . . . we don't care so much about user acquisition. If we get it, that's great from TikTok. We have other user acquisition channels that we obviously prioritize. TikTok is one of those places, it's like a playground for us at this point where we can have fun, test and learn, see what works and kind of build on that" (Doughty 2021). Overall, however, the article reports that this attitude has led to new users, new employees, and an overall deeper understanding of the brand's personality (IMC) and culture (corporate communication) as well as a desire to protect that brand authenticity.

More importantly, in a technological age, companies and brands *must* review the history of their communicative strategies, the ethical component to engaging with numerous audiences, the corporate culture associated with their companies, and the push in a technological age for different forms of communication. What Duolingo offers comes directly from Parvez herself: "If we get users to sign up for accounts, that's great, but it was never our objective" (Wong 2021). Mae Karwowski, who is the CEO of Obviously, a marketing agency, noted in the *NBC News* article that Duolingo has also maintained its successful status by "stay[ing] on top of trends" (Wong 2021). What this means is that, in corporate communication and IMC practices today, organizations must understand that the new landscape comes with new rules. Objectives through different channels are not always focused upon persuading for a purchase, intending to gain a profit. And audiences, who are impacted by brands whether or not they are traditional stakeholders, are acutely aware of the knowledge that companies and brands have about culture and trends.

The example of Duolingo is one among several companies and brands (for example Wendy's) that have adopted the desire to cultivate a different personality on social media rather than push a product or a service. In an *AdWeek* article by Catherine Perloff (July 2022), the publication noted that a "new class of social media managers is adopting a vernacular that diverges from the mother tongue of advertising." This new class is responsive to a changing communicative landscape that puts at risk that default to traditional models of corporate communication, advertising, and marketing.

Importantly, and as demonstrated by the Duolingo and TikTok example, companies and brands communication initiatives no longer can simply rely on knowing their traditional audiences and stakeholders. A company and brand's messages are being received by audiences beyond traditional stakeholders in significant numbers and with significant impact in a technological age. Though Duolingo does in fact create content that is meant to resonate with its traditional audiences, these new communication technologies and social media platforms create spaces where audiences extending beyond these traditional stakeholders are impacted by the message. Even more so than promoting the brand, Duolingo's misstep generated immediate impact

amongst audiences that were not part of traditional stakeholders. And, con-
versely, Duolingo's branding efforts on TikTok also reach audiences that
extend beyond those that either utilize Duolingo's app or follow its social
media content exclusively. Ever since the rise of corporate communication
and IMC, expectations from audiences have fundamentally shifted and created a new strategic rulebook in engaging with audiences that companies and
brands must respond to and engage with to continue to build relationships and
have positive impacts in this historical moment.

Conclusion

Engaging Audiences beyond Stakeholders in a Technological Age

The current communicative landscape that our culture and global society finds itself within is the product of decades of development and social shifts. Because of this, communicative practices like corporate communication and IMC are without choice. Companies and brands must respond to the environment or risk losing their traditional stakeholders. However, and importantly in this historical moment, traditional stakeholders are not the only audiences listening to companies and brands nor are they alone in being impacted by the messages that companies and brands strategically communicate to the public. In a technological age, the practices of corporate communication and IMC that have developed historically and that are protected culturally *must* be adapted to this changing environment. Through Duolingo's example, a company and brand that still persuades even when it is not actively persuading, offers a framework from which to understand audience expectations and a way to view the need to unite corporate communication and IMC in a technological age.

This work positioned corporate communication and IMC as two distinct practices with historical importance and strategic necessity that, when united, contribute importantly to a company's ability to engage with audiences beyond traditional stakeholders ethically and rhetorically in a complex communication environment. Authors Sundheim and Starr (2020) make note of stakeholder capitalism in an article for *Harvard Business Review*. Stakeholder capitalism, which the authors root in the 1950s and 1960s, was a "popular management theory" that "focused on the needs of all constituents, not just shareholders" (Sundheim and Starr 2020). For the authors, a new turn has been made in business practices that specifically attend to a new moment of attending to audiences beyond stakeholders as well as shareholders (Sundheim and Starr 2020). While Sundheim and Starr dive into the important financial implications of a move beyond immediate *shareholders*, their message is important in that business communication practices must extend beyond traditional understandings (whether of shareholders, stakeholders, or audience members) as these changing definitions have significant impact but also will not see immediate response in the marketplace (Sundheim and Starr 2020). This narrative is essential to accommodate important environmental and sustainability factors in business practices.

Aksoy et al. (2022) also refer back to stakeholder capitalism in noting that there exists "heightened calls" for the necessity to "address the needs of multiple stakeholders, not just shareholders" (445). This new "emphasis," furthermore, "demands that firms actively engage with a much larger and disparate group of stakeholders, each with distinct needs and objectives" (446). For Aksoy et al. (2022), depending upon a number of different scholars to form their analysis, stakeholders can be considered as those that advance the company or brand position in the marketplace (446). This is important for marketing functions as well, in that stakeholders are also "cocreators of value" and, with this influence, can offer insight into the marketplace (447). The authors also directly draw attention to the changes that communication technologies have introduced in these relationships, granting influence to several audiences. Consequently, this means that companies and brands have a direct responsibility to acknowledge that influence.

These implications also see common threads in IMC scholarship. Importantly, definitional clarity of all terms is a necessary step forward in being capable of implementing these changes and suggestions. For example, Mortimer and Laurie (2017) begin their scholarly inquiry into the state of IMC today by making note that "there is now acceptance by many academic and practitioners that integrated marketing communication (IMC) is the way forward in this complex multi-platform digital environment in which we now operate" (511). The authors suggest, however, that a number of barriers exist to implementing IMC at the corporate level, specifically when it comes to internal acceptance of the practice, including definitional clarity of IMC itself, complex corporate structures that naturally create barriers to changing communication strategies, a misperception of IMC that it requires a central-ized department or person, and, finally, an overall lack of connection between brand identity and reputation that is accurately accounted for in the IMC process, particularly when inviting third parties into the process (515). In light of their enumerated barriers to successful IMC implementation, which the authors suggest is *needed*, strong corporate communication practices that recognize the essential role that IMC plays in corporate livelihood becomes an initial starting place for meeting the demands of this historical moment and communicating with audiences that transcend traditional stakeholders—unit-ing corporate communication and IMC.

Killian and McManus (2015) note that the "proliferation of social media has instigated a revolution in the communications field, resulting in consumers expecting the brand to interact with them in a medium where the consumer controls every aspect of the conversation" (540). In a technological age, which has ushered in the need to engage with audiences beyond stakeholders, a communicative shift has altered who controls the message and influences outcomes. Yet companies and brands exert influence over how a brand is perceived through an integration of thoughtful communication directed toward and with audiences that reflects back on the corporate mission, values, and identity. The example of Duolingo offers a clear framing on how powerful companies can truly be with audiences when they meet the demands of the communicative environment as well as the needs of their various audiences while simultaneously returning to their values and identity.

As we continue to acknowledge the shifting demands of traditional stakeholders, corporate communication and IMC practices, when united, are also capable of meeting needs of audiences that transcend stakeholders immediate to the company or the brand. In Duolingo's example, the cultivation of a public presence of a social media platform, lacking a blatant message of product promotion, carries with it important implications for audience adaptation. In today's historical moment, the use of technology platforms (e.g., social media) implies a reach extending far beyond traditional stakeholders. Any human being may count as an audience that receives a message. Moreover, the structure of the platform itself provides a place where persuasion centered around product or service is not enough. Instead, persuasion must also rely upon corporate value and identity, evoking the absolute necessity of clear, concise, and strategic corporate communication.

Without doubt, the unification of corporate communication and IMC has begun to gain academic and scholarly inquiry and emphasis. For example, Alwi et al. (2022) promote the term "integrated hybrid communication" to emphasize the need to unite these two communication strategies in the current technological environment. The authors note that, though IMC purports an outside-in approach, strong corporate communication that recognizes the "strategic importance" that employees carry creates an environment through which employees can "effectively diffus[e] the corporate vision, mission, and goals" (410). Moreover, citing a number of scholars, the authors recognize that to try IMC as simply a "marketing device rather than a strategic business process" creates a "consumer orientation type of communication rather than stakeholder orientation" (410). The goal in this communication environment for both corporate communication and IMC is one and the same. Companies and brands strive to build relationships with audiences, and that presupposes that relationships exist with a number of different audiences that extend beyond traditional definitions.

Alwi et al. (2022) note that companies and brands must ensure that all communication, both internally and externally, emphasize corporate and brand identity, evolving from the beginning of a company's founding, which significantly contributes to one of IMC's overarching goals of "brand awareness" (415). But, importantly, the authors also note that once a company is clear in this strategy, then that company can be more effective in relationship building, another important element of IMC (416). Through emphasizing the interconnectedness between identity, values, and branding, the authors suggest that it is increasingly becoming more difficult to distinguish between corporate communication and IMC practices. Thus, philosophically, uniting the two practices or, at least, recognizing the interplay between the two, allows for better engagement of all audiences who are impacted by messages.

When a company understands and embodies, to its core, its proposed values, mission, and identity, corporate communication ensures a strategic approach to relationship maintenance with internal and external stakeholders that solidifies a common ground for *internal* audiences to engage with and to then move into messaging in the public sphere. Moreover, in a complex communication environment, understanding values permits an engagement of audiences that is unique to organizational mission, and textures communication strategy. Branding activities and IMC practices that are already transcending stakeholders can subsequently allow for messaging and communication strategies that take seriously the rhetorical call from audiences to provide an ethical engagement for two-way communication that is central to corporate communication and IMC in the twenty-first century.

While there are true differences between corporate communication and IMC, the synergy that emerges when uniting the two areas reveals the impact companies and brands can have on human beings through communication. A noteworthy example of uniting corporate communication and IMC comes from the response by a company/brand during a moment of global uncertainty. On March 1, 2022, almost two years to the date stay-at-home orders were issued during the Covid-19 pandemic, Camilla Han-He (2022), a senior product manager at LinkedIn, posted a blog titled: "Why It's Time to Rewrite the Narrative on Career Breaks." The post announced a new feature that provided LinkedIn users with thirteen options to describe reasons for employment gaps. Han-He (2022) wrote, "Today, we're [LinkedIn is] introducing new tools and resources to help people re-enter the workforce after taking a career break." The post went on to discuss how LinkedIn is "introducing a new way to represent a career break in the Experience section of your LinkedIn Profile, with options like caregiving and health and well-being" (Han-He 2022). While the functional goal was to allow users to "highlight" how "life experiences can apply to prospective jobs," in adding the career gap option for users, LinkedIn also took a step towards helping to "de-stigmatize taking time away from work" (Han-He 2022). This example is a reflection of branding, and, more specifically, reflecting how human beings are branded through personal branding and (right or wrong) by companies and brands. The example also demonstrates the unification of corporate communication and IMC by a company or brand. On one hand, LinkedIn is using corporate communication to engage users and companies and brands alike. On the other hand, this is also IMC for LinkedIn because it is allowing for audiences beyond current users to see that there is a way for them to also communicate on the LinkedIn platform and to give it a chance.

Companies and brands can unite corporate communication and IMC by better understanding the human communication relationships people have with them in a technological age—reaching audiences beyond traditional stakeholders. As we have suggested, the move to attending to audiences beyond traditional stakeholders can be strengthened through the integration of corporate communication and IMC. Companies and brands will continue to increasingly use technology to communicate with audiences. From a traditional corporate communication framework, companies and brands may have good intentions in disseminating messages, but those intentions do not translate to behavior. Consequently, this also does not matter to an audience. Companies and brands *must* understand that corporate communication cannot be in one corner and IMC in the other. In uniting corporate communication and IMC, when companies and brands are communicating with different audiences (e.g., employees, shareholders, customers, consumers), particularly in a technological environment, opportunities exist to create strong branding *and* strong communication practices that continue to build and foster relationships, truly attending to audiences beyond stakeholders.

Bibliography

"About," OpenAI. Accessed February 16, 2023. https://openai.com/about/.

Aksoy, Lerzan, Sandhya Banda, Colleen Harmeling, Timothy L. Keiningham, and Anita Pansari. "Marketing's Role in Multi-Stakeholder Engagement." *International Journal of Research in Marketing* 39 (2022): 445–61.

Allyn, Bobby. "Here Are 4 Key Points from the Facebook Whistleblower's Testimony on Capitol Hill." *NPR online.* October 5, 2021. https://www.npr.org/2021/10/05/1043377310/facebook-whistleblower-frances-haugen-congress.

Alwi, Sharifah Faridah Syed, John M. T. Balmer, Maria-Cristina Stoian, and Philip J. Kitchen. "Introducing Integrated Hybrid Communication: The Nexus Linking Marketing Communication and Corporate Communication." *Qualitative Market Research: An International Journal* 25, no. 4 (2022): 405–32.

Arenci, Canberk. "IKEA Encourages People to #StayHome." *Digital Agency Network.* March 27, 2020. https://digitalagencynetwork.com/ikea-encourages-people-to-stay-home/.

Arendt, Hannah. *The Human Condition.* (Chicago: University of Chicago Press, 1958).

Argenti, Paul A. "Corporate Communication as a Discipline: Toward a Definition." *Management Communication Quarterly* 10, no. 1 (1996): 73–97.

Argenti, Paul A. "How Technology Has Influenced the Field of Corporate Communication." *Journal of Business and Technical Communication* 20, no. 3 (2006): 357–70.

Aristotle. *Nicamachean Ethics.* Trans. M. Ostwald. (Indianapolis, IN: Hackett Publishing Company, Inc., 1999).

Aristotle. (Antiquity). *On Rhetoric: A Theory of Civic Discourse.* Trans. George A. Kennedy. 2nd ed. (Oxford University Press, 2007).

Arnett, Ronald C. *Dialogic Confessions: Bonhoeffer's Rhetoric of Responsibility.* (Carbondale: Southern Illinois Press, 2005).

Arnett, Ronald C., and Pat Arneson. *Dialogic Civility in a Cynical Age: Community, Hope and Interpersonal Relationships.* (State University of New York Press, 1999).

Arnett, Ronald C., Janie M. Harden Fritz, and Leanne M. Bell. *Communication Ethics Literacy: Dialogue and Difference* (Sage, 2009).

Bagozzi, Richard P. "Reflections on Relationship Marketing in Consumer Markets." *Journal of the Academy of Marketing Science* 23, no. 4 (1995): 272–77.

Bartholomew, Mark. *AdCreep: The Case Against Modern Marketing.* (Stanford University Press, 2017).

Belasen, Alan T., and Ariel R. Belasen. "The Strategic Value of Integrated Corporate Communication: Functions, Social Media, and Stakeholders." *International Journal of Strategic Communication* 13, no. 5 (2019): 367–84.

Bellah, Robert N., Richard Madsen, William M. Sullivan, Ann Swidler, and Steven M. Tipton. *Habits of the Heart: Individualism and Commitment in American Life.* (University of California Press, 2008).

Blakeman, Robyn. *Integrated Marketing Communication: Creative Strategy from Idea to Implementation.* 3rd ed. (Rowman & Littlefield, 2018).

Bok, Sissela. *Common Values.* (Columbia: University of Missouri Press, 1995).

Book Flights, Make Reservations & Plan a Trip. Southwest Airlines. (n.d.). October 6, 2022. https://www.southwest.com/.

Bowen, Howard R. *Social Responsibilities of the Businessman.* (University of Iowa Press, 1953).

Bradley, Diana. "Social Media Managers Urge Understanding for One of Their Own After Duolingo Deletes Amber Heard Joke on TikTok." *PR Week.* May 19, 2022. https://www.prweek.com/article/1756612/social-media-managers-urge-understanding-one-own-duolingo-deletes-amber-heard-joke-tiktok.

Braze. "How 'Human' Is Your Brand?" May 10, 2019. https://www.forbes.com/sites/braze/2019/05/10/how-human-is-your-brand/?sh=6b491bc51219.

Browne, Ryan. "All You Need to Know about ChatGPT, the A.I. Chatbot That's Got the World Talking and Tech Giants Clashing." *CNBC online.* February 8, 2023. https://www.cnbc.com/2023/02/08/what-is-chatgpt-viral-ai-chatbot-at-heart-of-microsoft-google-fight.html.

Bruhn, Manfred, and Stefanie Schnebelen. "Integrated Marketing Communication— From Instrumental to a Consumer-centric Perspective." *European Journal of Marketing* 51, no. 3 (2015): 464–89.

Capoot, Ashley, and Sofia Pitt. "Google, Microsoft, Amazon and Other Tech Companies Have Laid Off More Than 70,000 Employees in the Last Year." *Wall Street Journal* online. January 18, 2023. https://www.cnbc.com/2023/01/18/tech-layoffs-microsoft-amazon-meta-others-have-cut-more-than-60000.html.

Carroll, Archie B. "The Four Faces of Corporate Citizenship." *Business and Society Review* 100, no. 1 (1998): 1–7.

Carroll, Archie B. "A History of Corporate Social Responsibility: Concepts and Practices." In A. M. Andrew Crane, D. Matten, J. Moon, & D. Siegel (Eds.), *The Oxford Handbook of Corporate Social Responsibility.* (New York: Oxford University Press, 2008).

Carroll, Archie B. "Corporate Social Responsibility: The Centerpiece of Competing and Complementary Frameworks." *Organizational Dynamics* 44, no. 2 (2015): 87–96.

CBS News. "After 20 Years, British Airways Returns to Pittsburgh, Offering Non-Stop Flights to London." *CBS News.* March 27, 2019.

Cheng, Andria. "How Wendy's Learned to Stop Worrying and Love Its Twitter Roasts of McDonald's." *Forbes Magazine*. October 8, 2018. https://www.forbes .com/sites/andriacheng/2018/10/08/wendys-twitter-roasts-have-become-the-envy -of-marketers-heres-how-it-does-it/?sh=12987beefea4.

Chouinard, Yvon. "Earth Is Now Our Only Shareholder." *Patagonia*. 2022. https:// www.patagonia.com/home/.

Christensen, Lars Thøger, Mette Morsing, and George Cheney. *Corporate Communications: Convention, Complexity and Critique*. (Sage, 2008).

Christensen, Lars Thøger, Simon Torp, and A. Firat. "Integrated Marketing Communication and Postmodernity: An Odd Couple." *Corporate Communications: An International Journal* 10, no. 2 (2005): 156–67.

Clark, Travis. "Kylie Jenner and Kim Kardashian Tell Instagram to 'Stop Trying to Be Tiktok,' Which Could Spell Major Trouble for the Platform." *Business Insider*. September 24, 2022. https://www.businessinsider.com/kylie-jenner-kim -kardashian-instagram-stop-trying-to-be-tiktok-2022-7.

Collins, Jim. *Good to Great and the Social Sectors*. (Harper Business, 2005).

Coombs, W. Timothy, and J. Sherry Holladay. "The Paracrisis: The Challenges Created by Publicly Managing Crisis Prevention." *Public Relations Review* 38, no. 3 (2012): 409.

Cornelissen, Joep. "Corporate Image: An Audience Centered Model." *Corporate Communications: An International Journal*, no. 2 (2000): 119–25.

Cornelissen, Joep. *Corporate Communication: A Guide to Theory and Practice*. (Los Angeles: SAGE, 2017).

Corporation. In *Oxford English Dictionary*. N.d. https://www.oed.com/view/Entry /41833.

Cova, Bernard. "The Postmodern Explained to Managers: Implications for Marketing." *Business Horizons* 39, no. 6 (1996): 15–23.

Coyle, Daniel. *The Culture Code: The Secrets of Highly Successful Groups*. (Bantam, 2018).

CVS Health. "CVS Caremark Announces Corporate Name Change to CVS Health to Reflect Broader Healthcare Commitment." September 3, 2014. https://www .cvshealth.com/news-and-insights/press-releases/cvs-caremark-announces -corporate-name-change-to-cvs-health-to.

Daniels, Colin. "Language Learning App Duolingo Shares Why Tiktok Loves Its Green Owl." *AdWeek online*. September 13, 2022. https://www.adweek.com/social -marketing/language-learning-app-duolingo-shares-why-tiktok-loves-its-green -owl/.

Davies, Rob, and Simon Goodley. "Uber Bosses Told Staff to Use 'Kill Switch' during Raids to Stop Police Seeing Data." July 10, 2022. https://www.theguardian.com /news/2022/jul/10/uber-bosses-told-staff-use-kill-switch-raids-stop-police-seeing -data.

Deal, Terrence E., and Allan A. Kennedy. *Corporate Cultures: The Rites and Rituals of Corporate Life*. (New York: Pereus, 2000).

Doughty, Nate. "By Learning the Language of Tiktok, Duolingo Soars to New Heights." *BizJournals*. November 4, 2021. https://www.bizjournals.com/pittsburgh/inno/stories/news/2021/11/04/how-duolingo-learned-the-language-of-tik-tok.html.

Douglas, Mary, and Baron C. Isherwood. *The World of Goods: Towards an Anthropology of Consumption*. (New York: Basic Books, 1996).

Duncan, Thomas R. *IMC: Using Advertising and Promotion to Build Brands*. (McGraw-Hill, 2002).

Duolingo. "Efficacy at Duolingo." *Duolingo*. September 24, 2022. https://www.duolingo.com/efficacyGeorgiadis, C. (2022, May 19).

"Edelman Trust 10." *Edelman online*. September 29, 2022. https://www.edelman.com/trust.

Fisher, Walter R. *Human Communication as Narration: Toward a Philosophy of Reason, Value, and Action*. (University of South Carolina Press, 1989).

Frank, Allan D., and Judi Brownell. *Organizational Communication and Behavior: Communicating to Improve Performance*. (Orlando, FL: Holt, Rinehart and Winston, 1989).

Freeman, R. Edward. *Strategic Management: A Stakeholder Approach*. (Cambridge University Press, 2010).

Friedman, Milton. *Capitalism and Freedom*. (University Press of Chicago, 1962).

Fritz, Janie Harden. *Professional Civility: Communicative Virtue at Work*. (New York: Peter Lang, 2013).

Gallup. "Quiet Quitting: In Most Cases, It Isn't Laziness." YouTube Video, 5:40. October 7, 2022, https://www.youtube.com/watch?v=ACjz5su7ffo&t=7s.

Georgiadis, Candice. "How Brands Are Capitalizing Tiktok to Win New Audiences." *Entrepreneur*. September 24, 2022. https://www.entrepreneur.com/science-technology/how-brands-are-capitalizing-tiktok-to-win-new-audiences/424961.

Gordon, Ross. "Unlocking the Potential of Upstream Social Marketing." *European Journal of Marketing* 47, no. 9 (2013): 1525–47.

Groom, S. Alyssa. "Integrated Marketing Communication: Anticipating the 'Age of Engage.'" *Communication Research Trends* 7, no. 4 (2008).

Grunig, James E. "A Situational Theory of Publics: Conceptual History, Recent Challenges and New Research." In D. Moss, T. MacManus, and D. Vercic (Eds.), *Public Relations Research: An International Perspective*. (London: Thomson, 1997).

Haas, Tanni. "Public Relations Between Universality and Particularity: Toward a Moral-Philosophical Conception of Public Relations Ethics." In Robert L. Heath (Ed.), *Handbook of Public Relations*. (London: Sage Publications, Inc., 2001).

Haberman, Clyde. "How an Unsolved Mystery Changed the Way We Take Pills." *The New York Times* online. September 16, 2018. https://www.nytimes.com/2018/09/16/us/tylenol-acetaminophen-deaths.html.

Han-He, Camilla. "Why It's Time to Rewrite the Narrative on Career Breaks." LinkedIn, March 1, 2022. https://www.linkedin.com/pulse/why-its-time-rewrite-narrative-career-breaks-camilla-han-he/.

Harris, Lloyd C. "Cultural Domination: They Key to Market-Oriented Culture?" *European Journal of Marketing* 32, no. 3/4 (1998): 354–73.

Harter, Jim. "Is Quiet Quitting Real?" *Gallup.com.* September 6, 2022. https://www .gallup.com/workplace/398306/quiet-quitting-real.aspx.

Hartley, Bob, and Dave Pickton. "Integrated Marketing Communications Requires a New Way of Thinking." *Journal of Marketing Communications* 5, no. 2 (1999): 97–106.

Hatch, Mary Jo, and Majken Schultz. "Relations between Organizational Culture, Identity, and Image." *European Journal of Marketing* 31, no. 5–6 (1997): 356–65.

Havelock, Eric A. *Preface to Plato.* (Cambridge, MA: The Belknap Press of Harvard University, 1963).

Heald, Morrell. *The Social Responsibilities of Business: Company and Community 1900–1960.* (Pr. of Case Western Reserve Univ., 1970).

"Help Center." Airbnb. Accessed February 16, 2023. https://www.airbnb.com/help/ article/13.

Henninger, Claudia Elisabeth, Panayiota J. Alevizou, and Caroline J. Oates. "IMC, Social Media, and UK Fashion Micro-organisations." *European Journal of Marketing* 51, no. 3 (2017): 668–91.

Hernandez-Fernandez, Asuncion, and Mathieu Collin Lewis. "Brand Authenticity Leads to Perceived Value and Trust." *European Journal of Management and Business Economics* 28, no. 3 (2019): 222–38.

Holt, Douglas. "Branding in the Age of Social Media: A Better Alternative to Branded Content." *Harvard Business Review.* March 2016. https://hbr.org/2016/03/branding -in-the-age-of-social-media.

Honigman, Brian. "How Duolingo Built a Successful $250 Million Brand by Being Kind of a Jerk." *Fast Company.* April 26, 2022. https://www.fastcompany.com /90741819/how-duolingo-built-a-250-million-brand-by-being-kind-of-a-jerk.

Humphries, Daniel. "Culture Is the DNA of the Company: An Interview with Jet Blue's SVP of Talent, Rachel Mccarthy." *Indeed online.* August 8, 2017. https:// www.indeed.com/lead/culture-is-dna-company-interview-jetblue.

Iglesias, Oriol, Alfons Sauquet, and Jordi Montaña. "The Role of Corporate Culture in Relationship Marketing." *European Journal of Marketing* 45, no. 4 (2011): 631–50.

IKEA. "Ikea 'Stay Home' Catalog: Family Boredom Solutions." (N.d.) https: //www.adsoftheworld.com/campaigns/ikea-stay-home-catalog-family-boredom -solutions.

Johansen, Trine Susanne, and Sophie Esmann Andersen. "Co-creating ONE: Rethinking Integration Within Communication." *Corporate Communications: An International Journal* (2012).

Johnstone, Christopher Lyle. "Ethics, Wisdom, and the Mission of Contemporary Rhetoric: The Realization of Human Being." *Central States Speech Journal* 32 (1981): 177–88.

Jones, Thomas M. "Corporate Social Responsibility Revisited, Redefined." *California Management Review* 22, no. 3 (1980): 59–67.

Kamal, Jenna. "6 of the Best Marketing Campaigns You Need to See in 2022." *GWI.* April 14, 2022. https://blog.gwi.com/marketing/10-powerful-examples-of -marketing-that-works/.

Kant, Immanuel. *Critique of Judgement.* Trans. J. H. Bernard. (London: New York: Macmillan & Co., 1892).

Kaplan, Juliana, and Madison Hoff. "Americans Are Still Saying 'I Quit' in Near-Record Numbers Showing That the Great Resignation Is Sticking Around." *Business Insider.* June 1, 2022. https://www.businessinsider.com/americans-quit-at -near-record-rate-great-resignation-forever-resignation-2022-6.

Kelly, Lora. "Senate Announces Hearing After Chaos over Taylor Swift Ticket Sales." *New York Times.* November 22, 2022. https://www.nytimes.com/2022/11 /22/business/senate-antitrust-ticketmaster-taylor-swift.html.

Kerr, Gayle, Don Schultz, Charles Patti, and Ilchul Kim. "An Inside-Out Approach to Integrated Marketing Communication: An International Analysis." *International Journal of Advertising* 27, no. 4 (2008): 511–48.

Key, Thomas Martin, and Andrew J. Czaplewski. "Upstream Social Marketing Strategy: An Integrated Marketing Communications Approach." *Business Horizons* 60 (2017): 325–33.

Killian, Ginger, and Kristy McManus. "Marketing Communications Approach for the Digital Era: Managerial Guidelines for Social Media Integration." *Business Horizons* 58 (2015): 539–49.

Kliatchko, Jerry. "Revisiting the IMC Construct: A Revised Definition and Four Pillars." *International Journal of Advertising* 27, no. 1 (2008): 133–60.

Kuhn, Thomas. *The Structure of Scientific Revolution.* 3rd ed. (University of Chicago Press, 1996).

Landau, Elizabeth. "CVS Stores to Stop Selling Tobacco." 2014. https://www.cnn .com/2014/02/05/health/cvs-cigarettes/index.html.

Lantos, Geoffrey P. "The Boundaries of Strategic Corporate Social Responsibility." *Journal of Consumer Marketing* 18, no. 7 (2001): 595–632.

Latapí Agudelo, Mauricio Andrés, Lára Jóhannsdóttir, and Brynhildur Davidsdóttir. "A Literature Review of The History and Evolution of Corporate Social Responsibility." *International Journal of Corporate Social Responsibility* 4, no. 1 (2019): 1–23. https://doi.org/10.1186/s40991-018-0039-y.

Laurie, Sally, and Kathleen Mortimer. "How to Achieve True Integration: The Impact of Integrated Marketing Communication on the Client/Agency Relationship." *Journal of Marketing Management* 35, no. 3/4 (2019): 231–52.

Lucas, Amelia. "Here's a Map of Starbucks Stores That Voted to Unionize." *CNBC online.* December 9, 2022. https://www.cnbc.com/2022/12/09/map-of-starbucks -stores-that-voted-to-unionize.html#:~:text=Unionizing%20at%20Starbucks ,voted%20to%20unionize%20since%202021.&text=A%20year%20ago%2C %20workers%20at,a%20first%20for%20the%20chain.

Luck, Edwina, and Jennifer Moffatt. "IMC: Has Anything Really Changed? A New Perspective on an Old Definition." *Journal of Marketing Communications* 15, no. 5 (2009): 311–25.

Luxton, Sandram, Mike Reid, and Felix Mavondo. "Integrated Marketing Communication Capability and Brand Performance." *Journal of Advertising* 44, no. 1 (2015): 37–46.

MacIntyre, Alasdair. *After Virtue: A Study of Moral Theory.* 3rd ed. (University of Notre Dame Press, 2007).

Madsbjerg, Christian, and Mikkel Rasmussen. *The Moment of Clarity.* (Boston: Harvard Business Review Press, 2014).

Maguire, Lucy. "Tarte's Dubai Backlash: Are Influencer Trips 'Tone Deaf' in 2023?" *Vogue Business.* January 20, 2023. https://www.voguebusiness.com/beauty/tartes -dubai-backlash-are-influencer-trips-tone-deaf-in-2023.

"M&Ms," About M&Ms, accessed on February 12, 2023. https://www.mms .com. M&Ms (@mmschocolate), "A message from M&Ms," *Twitter.* January 23, 2023. https://twitter.com/mmschocolate/status/1617518785686274052?cxt =HHwWilDQ5f-wyvIsAAAA.

"M&MS® Concludes Epic Super Bowl LVII Campaign." *PR Newswire online.* February 12, 2023. https://www.prnewswire.com/news-releases/mms-concludes -epic-super-bowl-lvii-campaign-301744789.html.

McCoy, Kimeko. "How Duolingo Is Using Its 'Unhinged Content' with Duo the Owl to Make People Laugh on TikTok." *Digiday.* December 13, 2021. https://digiday .com/marketing/how-duolingo-is-using-its-unhinged-content-with-duo-the-owl-to -make-people-laugh-on-tiktok/.

McDowell Marinchak, Christina L., and Jill Burk. "IMC Campaigns: Generating a Space for Civic Engagement." In J. Persuit and C. McDowell Marinchak (Eds.), *Integrated Marketing Communication: Creating Spaces for Engagement.* (Lanham, MD: Lexington Books, 2016).

Meikle, Scott. *Aristotle's Economic Thought.* (Clarendon Press, 1997).

Mendez II, Moises. "Why the Internet Became Fixated on an Influencer Trip to Dubai." *Time.* January 25, 2023. https://time.com/6249533/tarte-dubai-trip -influencer/.

Mortimer, Kathleen, and Sally Laurie. (2017). "The Internal and External Challenges Facing Clients in Implementing IMC." *European Journal of Marketing* 51, no. 3 (2017): 511–27.

Mueller, Julia, "Leaked 'Uber Files' Show How Company Capitalized on Violence against Drivers." *The Hill online.* July 10, 2022. https://thehill.com/policy /technology/3551750-leaked-uber-files-show-how-company-capitalized-on -violence-against-drivers/.

Munter, Mary. *Guide to Managerial Communication.* (Englewood, NJ: Prentice Hall, 1992).

NBC Chicago. "Tylenol Murders Investigation Sees Renewed Effort to Solve Case, 40 Years Later." *NBC Chicago.* September 22, 2022. https://www.nbcchicago.com/ investigations/tylenol-murders-investigation-sees-renewed-effort-to-solve-case-40 -years-later/2947573/.

O'Hara, Delia. "Kit Yarrow Is Unlocking Consumer Shopping Behavior." *American Psychological Association.* October 2, 2017. https://www.apa.org/members/content /yarrow-unlocking-shopping-behavior.

O'Kane, Caitlin. "M&Ms Puts Spokescandies on 'Indefinite Pause' in Wake of Uproar over Changes to Green M&M." January 23, 2023. https://www.cbsnews.com/news/mms-spokescandies-indefinite-pause-changes-green-mm-criticized-maya-rudolph-spokesperson/.

Oracle. "Consumer Views of Live Help Online 2012: A Global Perspective." *Oracle Retail.* March 2012. https://www.oracle.com/us/products/applications/commerce/live-help-on-demand/oracle-live-help-wp-aamf-1624138.pdf.

Ots, Mart, and Gergely Nyilasy. "Integrated Marketing Communications (IMC): Why Does It Fail?: An Analysis of Practitioner Mental Models Exposes Barriers of IMC Implementation." *Journal of Advertising Research* 55, no. 2 (2015): 132–45.

Ots, Mart, and Gergely Nyilasy. "Just Doing It: Theorizing Integrated Marketing Communication (IMC) Practices." *European Journal of Marketing* 51, no. 3 (2017): 490–510.

Parker, Kim, and Juliana Menasce. "Majority of Workers Who Quit a Job in 2021 Cite Low Pay, No Opportunities for Advancement, Feeling Disrespected." *Pew Research Center.* March 9, 2022. https://www.pewresearch.org/fact-tank/2022/03/09/majority-of-workers-who-quit-a-job-in-2021-cite-low-pay-no-opportunities-for-advancement-feeling-disrespected/.

Patagonia. "Beyond the Office: Out of the Landfill." *Patagonia.* N.d. https://www.patagonia.com/transitioning-away-from-logos.html.

Paton, Elizabeth, Vanessa Friedman, and Jessica Testa. "When High Fashion and QAnon Collide." *New York Times online.* December 2, 2022. https://www.nytimes.com/2022/11/28/style/balenciaga-campaign-controversy.html.

Pearce, Barnett W. *Making Social Worlds: A Communication Perspective.* (Wiley-Blackwell, 2007).

Perloff, Catherine. "Once a Liability, The Rogue Social Media Manager Is Now an Advertising Strategy." *AdWeek online.* July 25, 2022. https://www.adweek.com/media/once-a-liability-the-rogue-social-media-manager-is-now-an-advertising-strategy/.

Perrow, Charles. *Complex Organizations: A Critical Essay.* (Brattleboro, VT: Echo Points & Media Books, 2015). Print (Original work published 1986).

Persuit, Jeanne M. *Social Media and Integrated Marketing Communication: A Rhetorical Approach.* (New York: Lexington Books, 2013).

Pitrelli, Monica. "Travel Companies Are 'Greenwashing'—Here Are 3 Ways to Find Ones That Aren't." *CNBC online.* January 29, 2023. https://www.cnbc.com/2023/01/29/travel-greenwashing-how-to-find-sustainable-travel-companies.html.

Porcu, Lucia, Salvador del Barrio-Garcia, Juan Miguel Alcántara-Pilar, and Esmeralda Crespo-Almendros. "Do Adhocracy and Market Cultures Facilitate Firm-Wide Integrated Marketing Communication (IMC)?" *International Journal of Advertising* 36, no. 1 (2017): 121–41.

Porcu, Lucia, Salvador del Barrio-García, Philip J. Kitchen, and Marwa Tourky. "The Antecedent Role of a Collaborative vs. a Controlling Corporate Culture on Firm-Wide Integrated Marketing Communication and Brand Performance." *Journal of Business Research* 119 (2020): 435–43.

Porter, Michael E., and Mark R. Kramer. "Creating Shared Value." *Harvard Business Review*. (2011).

Postman, Neil. "The Reformed English Curriculum." In A. C. Eurich (Ed.), *High School 1980: The Shape of the Future in American Secondary Education.* (1970).

Postman, Neil. *Technopoly: The Surrender of Culture to Technology.* (Vintage, 1993).

Postman, Neil. "The Humanism of Media Ecology." *Proceedings of the Media Ecology Association* 1 (2000).

Press-Reynolds, Kieran. "'Absolutely Shocked': Try Guys Fans and a Crisis PR Expert on the Cheating Scandal and What's Next for the YouTubers." *Insider.* October 7, 2022. https://www.insider.com/try-guys-consensual-workplace-scandal -cheating-fans-reaction-crisis-communication-2022-10.

Putnam, Linda L., and Dennis K. Mumby (Eds.). *The SAGE Handbook of Organizational Communication: Advances in Theory, Research, and Methods.* 3rd ed. (Sage, 2013).

Qin, Yufan Sunny, Marcia W. DiStaso, Alexis Fitzsimmons, Eve Heffron, and Linjuan Rita Men. "How Purpose-Driven Organizations Influenced Corporate Actions and Employee Trust during the Global COVID-19 Pandemic." *International Journal of Strategic Communication* 16, no. 3 (2022): 426–43.

Rearick, Lauren. "Duolingo TikTok: Meet the Social Media Coordinator behind Those Viral Videos." *Teen Vogue.* March 5, 2022. https://www.teenvogue.com/ story/duolingo-tiktok.

Rehman, Shakeel ul, Rafia Gulzar, and Wajeeha Aslam. "Developing the Integrated Marketing Communication (IMC) through Social Media (SM): The Modern Marketing Communication Approach." *Sage Open.* 2022.

Rushkoff, Douglas. *Present Shock: When Everything Happens Now.* (Current, 2013).

Schein, Edgar H., and Peter Schein. *Organizational Culture and Leadership.* 5th ed. (Wiley, 2016).

Schrag, Calvin O. *Communicative Praxis and the Space of Subjectivity.* (Purdue University Press, 1986).

Schultz, Don E., and Heidi F. Schultz. *IMC: The Next Generation.* (New York: McGraw-Hill, 2004).

Schultz, Don E., Stanley I. Tannenbaum, and Robert F. Lauterborn. *Integrated Marketing Communications: Putting It Together and Making It Work.* (New York: McGraw-Hill, 1993).

SEC. "SEC Charges Kim Kardashian for Unlawfully Touting Crypto Security. U.S. Securities and Exchange Commission." *Press Release.* October 3, 2022. https:// www.sec.gov/news/press-release/2022-183.

Shirky, Clay. *Here Comes Everybody: The Power of Organizing without Organizations.* (Penguin Books. 2008).

Simões, Claudia, and Roberta Sebastiani. "The Nature of the Relationship between Corporate Identity and Corporate Sustainability: Evidence from the Retail Industry." *Business Ethics Quarterly* 27, no. 3 (2017): 423–53.

Sisodia, Rajendra, David Wolfe, and Jagdish N. Sheth. *Firms of Endearment: How World-Class Companies Profit from Passion and Purpose.* (FT Press, 2007).

Spiers, Elizabeth. "Layoffs by Email Show What Employers Really Think of Their Workers." *New York Times online.* January 29, 2023. https://www.nytimes.com /2023/01/29/opinion/mass-tech-layoffs-email-google.html.

Sprout Social. "Social Media Trends for 2022 & Beyond." N.d. https://sproutsocial .com/insights/index/.

Strate, Lance. "Media Ecology 101: An Introductory Reading List. Media Ecology Association." 2019. https://www.media-ecology.org/Media-Ecology-101.

Strate, Lance. "What Is Media Ecology?" Media Ecology Association. N.d. https:// www.media-ecology.org/What-Is-Media-Ecology.

Sundheim, Doug, and Kate Starr. "Making Stakeholder Capitalism a Reality." *Harvard Business Review online.* January 22, 2020. https://hbr.org/2020/01/making -stakeholder-capitalism-a-reality.

Taylor, Charles. *Sources of the Self: The Making of the Modern Identity.* (Harvard University Press, 1989).

Taylor, Chloe. "M&Ms Are Taking 'an Indefinite Pause' from Their Iconic Spokescandies after Update to the Characters 'Broke the Internet.'" *Fortune online.* January 24, 2023. https://fortune.com/2023/01/24/mandms-taking-indefinite-pause -iconic-spokescandies-updates-characters-broke-internet/.

Ticketmaster (@Ticketmaster). "Due to Extraordinarily High Demands on Ticketing Systems and Insufficient Remaining Ticket Inventory to Meet That Demand, Tomorrow's Public On-Sale for Taylor Swift | The Eras Tour Has Been Canceled." *Twitter.* November 17, 2022, https://twitter.com/Ticketmaster/status /1593333211769106433?lang=en.

Tindale, Christopher W. "Rhetorical Argumentation and the Nature of Audience: Toward an Understanding of Audience—Issues in Argumentation." *Philosophy & Rhetoric* 46, no. 4 (2013): 508–32.

Trapp, N. Leila. "Corporation as Climate Ambassador: Transcending Business Sector Boundaries in a Swedish CSR Campaign." *Public Relations Review* 38, no. 3 (2012): 458–65.

Turkle, Sherry. *Reclaiming Conversation: The Power of Talk in a Digital Age.* (Penguin Press, 2015).

Turner, Gregory B., and Barbara Spencer. "Understanding the Marketing Concept as Organizational Culture." *European Journal of Marketing* 31, no. 2 (1994): 110–21.

Van Riel, Cees B. M., and Charles J. Fombrun. *Essential of Corporate Communication: Implementing Practices for Effective Reputation Management.* (London: Routledge, 2007).

Vaughn, Aidan. "Brands Being Unhinged on Social Media Works: Duolingo Will Find You." *Marketing Magazine.* August 26, 2022. https://www.marketingmag.com.au /featured/brands-being-unhinged-on-social-media-works-duolingo-will-find-you/.

Wankel, Charles. *21st Century Management: A Reference Handbook.* (SAGE Publications, 2008).

Waterhouse, Benjamin C. "The Personal, The Political and the Profitable: Business and Protest Culture, 1960s–1980s." *Financial History* 121 (2017): 14–17.

"We Believe That Ice Cream Can Change the World." Ben & Jerry's. (n.d.) February 15, 2023. https://www.benjerry.com/values/issues-we-care-about/climate-justice.

Weisskopf, Jean-Philippe, and Philippe Massett. "2022 Top Hospitality Industry Trends." *EHL Insights.* N.d. https://hospitalityinsights.ehl.edu/hospitaltiy-industry -trends.

"'We Will Not Make Excuses': Uber Responds to Uber Files Leak." *The Guardian.* July 10, 2022. https://www.theguardian.com/news/2022/jul/10/uber-response-uber -files-leak.

Wheless, Erika. "How Duolingo Conquered Brand TikTok." *AdAge online.* April 25, 2022. https://adage.com/article/special-report-agency-list-creativity-awards/ creativity-awards-2022-winner-duolingo/2410666.

Wong, Wilson. "How Duo the Big Green Owl Became a Tiktok Star." *NBC News.* November 4, 2021. https://www.nbcnews.com/pop-culture/pop-culture-news/duo -big-green-owl-became-tiktok-star-rcna4445.

Yarrow, Kit. *Decoding the New Consumer Mind: How and Why We Shop and Buy.* (John Wiley & Sons, 2014).

Zuckerberg, Mark. "I Want to Share a Note I Wrote to Everyone at Our Company." *Facebook.* October 5, 2021. https://www.facebook.com/zuck/posts /10113961365418581.

Index

94

Index

About the Authors

Christina L. McDowell Marinchak (PhD, Duquesne University, 2012) teaches courses in business writing and persuasive communication as well as serves as a faculty advisor for corporate communication-related, community-engaged learning projects at Cornell University in the SC Johnson College of Business Nolan School of Hotel Administration. Her work has been published in journals such as *Western Journal of Communication*, *Communication Research Trends, The Journal of Learning Community Research and Practice*, and *Journal of the Association Communication Administration.* She is the co-editor and contributing author of *Integrated Marketing Communication: Creating Spaces for Engagement* (2016). Dr. McDowell Marinchak has delivered business and professional communication presentations and led workshops in industry on topics related to corporate communication, interpersonal communication, presentation skills, business writing, and generational communication in the workplace.

Sarah M. DeIuliis (PhD, Duquesne University, 2018) teaches courses in integrated marketing communication in the Department of Communication & Rhetorical Studies at Duquesne University. Dr. DeIuliis has published in journals such as *Southern Communication Journal*, *The Atlantic Journal of Communication, Communication Research Trends, Listening: Journal of Communication Ethics, Religion, and Culture,* and *Journal of the Association for Communication Administration.* She is a co-author of *Corporate Communication Crisis Leadership: Ethics and Advocacy* (2017).

Printed in the USA
CPSIA information can be obtained
at www.ICGtesting.com
LVHW042042280124
770155LV00002B/99

9 781498 566827